*WARNING:*

*BLIZZARD is
based on a true story.*

**What happened to 14-year-old
Michael Dowling should
have killed him.
But, incredibly,
it didn't.**

# BLIZZARD
## written by L R Lehmann

Copyright 1997 by QuikReadPress
All rights reserved

Distributed by Publishers Distribution
800 922-9681

Edited by Nettie T. Bagley & Faye Smith
Artwork by Ken Isaac

ISBN 0-9659758-0-0

Printed in the United States of America

# BLIZZARD

# L R LEHMANN

*For Kerry*
*Sean, Robbe*
*and Paul*

*The white monster with the fierce howling voice and the stinging tongue had taken that from him too,  and had only laughed with its frigid breath when he had uttered a simple "please."*

# PROLOGUE

"Nope, nope I don't think so," the old-timer in the quilted overalls, seated at the counter in the coffee shop on Highway 212 seemed sure of himself. "We've had some bad ones, but nuthin' like that one back in '27."

A man with a *"Land o' Lakes Feeds"* baseball hat was ready to challenge the statement. "How do you know Bill? You were only 'bout two years old then."

"So what! Everyone's heard about that one."

A pork-eating guy with a two-day, gray, stubble beard spoke next. "Hell, my dad would talk about that one for hours. He seemed to take a special pride in knowing he had survived it." He interrupted himself to summon an equally robust woman who appeared to have several pillows wedged under a greasy, pink dress. "Nancy, can you bring me just a little bit more o' that coffee?"

The four men relished this kind of conversation. Memories consumed most of their lives. Each would rather miss a Vikings football game than the daily meeting at the coffee shop.

The man in the overalls felt the urge to comment further. "Yeah, this year ain't been no tropical heat wave and the one back in '72 and even '47, they were bad ones. But from what I hear the blizzard of '27, yup that there blizzard they say could freeze a squirt of milk midway 'tween the cow and the bucket. That was about the worst one."

The oldest of the quartet, a man in his nineties who hadn't seen a razor in about a week, spoke next. He was irritated. "Lizzards, lizzards, hell I saw some lizzards out in Utah thirty, forty years ago... they weren't much. Sure not worth a whole damned conversation."

"No Floyd, not lizzards. We're talking

blizzards here, blizzards with a "b." Not lizzards, buh... lizzards, blizzards. The man in the feed cap was slighly annoyed. He continued speaking into his coffee cup as he drew it to his lips. "Lizzards, he thinks we're talking about lizzards here."

The 90-something-year-old was becoming more perturbed. "Well then I'll tell you about a blizzard. What about the one in '80?"

The man with the baseball cap spoke, "Eighty wasn't hardly anything at all. Wasn't that the year the river never even froze up all year?"

"Not nineteen eighty numbskull," the senior partner of the foursome was extremely irritated now. His face reddened and his pace quickened. "Eighteen eighty... Eighteen eighty. You guys haven't heard about that kid from over near Canby?"

The man in the overalls was annoyed. "Come on Floyd, eighteen eighty? We don't know anybody that was alive then, and neither do you."

He stopped, stifled a smile and felt the need to further aggravate the older man.

"Wait a second, just wait one second here. Floyd you weren't alive back then were you?"

"No, hell no I wasn't alive then," he felt a need to defend his youth. "Hadn't been born yet. I wasn't alive. I was... I was uh... dead!"

Dead? That's a novel thought. Is it possible that we were dead if we hadn't yet been born?

The boy, buried with his dog, wasn't dead, but he wasn't quite sure. And if he wasn't dead, then he probably would be soon. Death, he thought, was inevitable. He didn't want to die. He was only 14-years-old.

There were those who shook their heads, "It was a shame," they would say. "It's too bad he lived."

*A nervous kind of fright was beginning to replace the guilt Mike Dowling had been feeling. But fear was more foreign than courage, and he stepped into the chalk-marked circle.*

# CHAPTER ONE

E ven then buildings were tall and the narrow streets were filled with a mix of horses, buggies, cars, poles, tracks, wires and vendors hawking a variety of goods. People in the streets were a tangle of foreign accents and diverse appearances. Great ships and small boats maneuvered through the harbors and rivers. There was smoke and pollution.

Things haven't changed much since 1919.

The Hippodrome was one of those buildings that New Yorkers were smugly proud of. It had 5,697 seats. There were nights when sweat, smoke and screams boiled-over, out of the building and into the alleys and avenues as athletic events of seemingly great importance took place inside its brick walls. There were nights when the center stage held a more refined presentation, attracting those of culture and supposed good taste.

This Sunday night in late March was to be of the later genre.

Outside, surrounding the massive building, long rows of red cross ambulances lined the streets. A huge banner had been draped across the interior of the cavernous structure: "NY CHAPTER RED CROSS WELCOMES WW VETERANS." The five thousand, six hundred people in the Hippodrome talked loudly while moving toward their seats. Some hopped, some wheeled and some limped. Tonight, one thousand soldiers, all injured in the war, were the special guests of the Red Cross. Their seats, the front rows, directly in front of the stage, were reserved especially for them.

The parade of soldiers was slow.

Each veteran wore a special name tag that included his name and a large title that read: "Honored Guest-American Red Cross." It was evident to all, the name tags were superfluous. The guests of honor could easily be identified by their numerous slings, crutches, eye patches and wheelchairs.

Some of their faces mirrored pain and misery, but most were a study in quiet resolve. They had come to hear a message. The majority were skeptical. Their lives had become a blur of dull, gray days with little or no employment. For many the most menial tasks had become time consuming obstacles that stood in the way of sleep. There wasn't much else.

And yet, on the front rows in the Hippodrome there was an undeniable feeling of brotherhood. They perceived they had come to hear one of their own.

But was he?

Rumor had it that this night's speaker had never tasted the raw fear, the mud and the gun powder that was war. He had never served in the military. So how was it that he, a man who had never felt the pain of watching a buddy gunned down by an enemy that yelled and cursed in words not understood... how was he qualified to speak to them?

A young soldier was whispering to his neighbor. "Let's see what this guy's about?"

The bright, electric lights were switched off with an audible bang. Only a single spotlight remained. Silence fell upon the crowd. A man was walking towards the center of the huge wooden stage. Somewhere in the balcony a woman coughed. In the street an anonymous clanging bell was only barely perceptible.

"Ladies and gentlemen, Supreme Court Justice, The Honorable Charles Evans Hughes." There was a sprinkling of lazy applause as a man, looking somewhat like a banker, approached the huge, odd-looking microphone.

"The man you are about to meet should have died 39 years ago." Mr. Hughes spoke slowly and distinctly. " He is my friend and he is about to be yours. I present Mr. Michael John Dowling."

Semi-vigorous applause rippled through the Hippodrome. On the front rows there was a small spattering of obligatory hand clapping. A man on the second row with two crutches, turned to a friend and smiled. They were prepared to dislike this man. They had heard of this guy from Minnesota, but had never seen him. They were there because it was their payment, of sorts, for the free, roast beef dinner they had just consumed.

The bearded Dowling, 53-years-old and nervous, walked at a moderate pace to the microphone. He was somewhat uncomfortable with the clapping; and rather than wait for it to die down, he began speaking in a strong and sure voice. "Good Evening, I have a lot to tell you. I guess I'd better start at the beginning."

———

The Mississippi is a dirty river; brown as molasses but not quite as thick. A river boat can change all that. At least for a few brief seconds. *The Alexander Mitchell* paddled slowly toward berth 18 at St. Louis. It was a vivid, summer morning. The huge steamboat held a cargo of tired, sweating people and Louisiana cotton. The cotton was about to be transformed into the Missouri calico that the sweating passengers would wear on their next trip down river.

The magical act that made diamonds of muddy water happened at the huge paddle wheel attached to the rear of the vessel. The dark, cocoa liquid was pulled into the white paddles and, as it was tossed into the air, it became gloriously bright and clean in the brilliant sunshine. While it was magic, it was also monotonous.

Just as the first flowers of spring are met with excitement, the flowers that follow soon become mundane and are noticed by only a few. The action of the paddle on the water had ceased to be magic long ago for all of the crew and most of the passengers. Now, on this August morning, only two people watched; a man in his early thirties, and a young boy.

The man was there because the boy liked the show. The youngster was fascinated with the paddle, had watched it for hours and still found entertainment in its dance through the brown, watery floor. The man, dressed like the other workers on board, did what he could to entertain the kid. He felt he owed it to him.

The boy's thoughts were a turbulent mix of sweet and sour and warmth and cold.

The moment was good, but the immediate future left a nagging sensation of guilt that wouldn't go away. It was like the ever-present tickle in the throat of a person trying desperately to stifle a chronic cough.

*It's fun to come into the dock,* he thought, *but I know what I'll have ta do here and... it's fun, kind of fun, but I still wish it was over... wish we were heading out again.*

The boy wiped the spray from his forehead with the fingers of his right hand. The move of his hand continued through a shock of boyish blonde hair. "It's almost like diamonds, Pa! The water looks clean as fountain water fer a second or two."

"That it does Mikey, that it does."

Eleven-year-old Michael Dowling and his father squinted at the moving paddles in the bright sunshine.

"Well she'll be ready fer 'nloadin' in just a wee bit." John Dowling, the father was, in his own words, *poor but Irish.* "We best be gittin' o'er to the starbo'rd side, Mikey."

The elder Dowling was a hard drinking man. Income was never steady and when it arrived, its departure was always close behind. Young Michael had played the part of a nomad, wandering from town to town with his father since the death of his mother in Massachusetts one year before. It was an adventure made better by the love and concern of a father who wrestled with a huge animal of a conscience, always wanting to do the right thing for his young son, but sometimes failing.

"Hey Dowling, hey John, come over here!" It was Jack Sorley, an evil-looking grunt who had prowled the docks for 30 years. "Is Mikey with yuh on this trip?"

The boat had docked, and John Dowling was helping one other man put the gangway in place for the anxious passengers when Sorley approached.

"I think I got a live one for Mike for this afternoon. Some red-haired kid 'bout thirteen. Most of the guys are gonna bet on him. The word is he can beat Mikey. But I don't think so. We can make some dough. Whad' ya say?"

John Dowling didn't like Sorley. He had caught him cheating in a card game. It's not that he hated cheaters. He did it himself whenever he thought he could get away with it. But Sorley's cheating on that night in May had been detected by everyone but Dowling. He had felt stupid. But worse than that, he had lost thirty-eight dollars.

"Well Jack," Dowling was going to try for more than the standard fifty percent of the take. There almost always was a take. The younger Dowling had lost only once in thirteen fights. "Tell you what Jack, Mikey's not feelin' that good. I think we better pass."

Just then young Mike, with a splattered apron, appeared on an upper deck.

"Nonsense, he's a picture of health. The boy never looked finer. Look at him, John, the boy's eager for a good fight."

"Well, I dunno. Helpin' the cook... he's been... he's been a cookin' fer days, an' I think he's a bit famished, he is!" John Dowling wanted the fight, he wanted the money. He paused, looked up at his young son, probed at his left ear with a dirty finger and continued. "It's gonna take more than 'alf"

"How much ya want?"

"I want two-thirds o' the take."

The sloppy stevedore growled something obscene as a giant knob of brown tobacco juice flew from his lips and splashed with little dignity on the boardwalk near Dowling's left foot. He scratched at a scar near his left eye.

"All right then, two-thirds it is Dowling. Six o'clock then, right here."

Sorley's departure was quick. He walked directly to an oil-paper covered saloon not sixty paces away. John Dowling had been cheated again and Dowling almost halfway knew it.


The grizzled fight promoter, in a dark corner of the *River Bend Tavern,* was boasting to a drunken fisherman. "If the Dowlings wins, they'll get two-thirds of the take... of the known take. It ain't a smart thing for me to be puttin' all o' the money into that sorry hat. In fact," he jabbed the disinterested man, "in fact, I only put about half the money into that hat." He burst into a red-faced laugh, then became very serious. "And rightly so, I believe. I cover all of the losses, a risk like that is worth some extra money."

The younger Dowling finished his chores, scrubbing pots in the boat's cramped kitchen. His days were measured in stacks of black iron kettles coated with baked beans and griddles that wore skins of hardened fat. He worked hard.

He knew there were kids that wore clean pressed trousers and fancy striped shirts. He had seen them riding about the streets with bags of candy on their <u>own</u> bicycles. He often thought about being one of them, living in a big house near the river and going to the schools for "rich kids." There was no danger, he thought, in fantasizing.

But about the time his thought pattern reached the vision of himself in a fancy suit riding in a shiny carriage, something would always clang shut in his mind, and a grainy black and white picture would overtake his thoughts.

*What about the other kids... the ones who lived in the orphanage on Sterling Street? They don't go anywhere... prisoners of sort, no family at all! No steamboats, nothing! Them orphans are about the worst. Things aren't so bad for me!*

Dowling felt comfortable with being skinny. And the freckles, he figured they would go away one day, and just about every kid had them anyway. He knew he was a tough kid. His father had taught him how to fight. He fought well, but there was always that gnawing feeling of guilt. He liked being the victor but the queeze, before each fight, like a hard pill jammed under his tongue, made him uneasy.

The senior Dowling had entered the kitchen where Michael was hanging his dirty apron on a rusted nail.

"Pa, you know Mom wouldn' like it."

"I s'pose not Mikey. But she always said you were gon' ta be someone mighty importan' one day. An' the way I see it, you winnin' ev'ry time is kin' of importan' righ' now."

Slightly before 6 p.m., the two Dowlings approached the dock. The early evening shadows had created an occasional pool of refuge from the day's heat. *The Alexander Mitchell* had been joined by a new steamer: *The War Eagle.* The huge white boat was rocking in a slow cadence at berth 16. A few men were engaged in removing what appeared to be cages of noisy chickens from its rear deck.

Mike Dowling felt an immediate rush of excitement as he gazed upon the bigger boat. He and his Dad had signed to join *The War Eagle's* crew. On the new boat he would continue the monotony of peeling potatoes and scrubbing pots and pans, but a different boat was always a reason for excitement.

John Dowling engaged himself in a variety of chores to earn a paycheck. But his expertise was in carpentry and most of the boats had a need for one or two carpenters on board.

Near berth 18 at St. Louis, the real center of activity was Mr. Jack Sorley. A younger man was at Sorley's side, writing names and figures on a small tablet of paper. Sorley was snatching at handfuls of cash and stuffing it in a tattered, greasy bowler.

"It's gonna be a good one. Tony's a wiry lad, but my money's on Dowling." Sorley's loud statement was a rare truth for a man who didn't know the meaning of the word.

Tony Mannari, the 13-year old Italian kid looked suspiciously like he was 15. He had a good 10 inches on the 11-year old and used coarse words that even produced an occasional raised eyebrow on the grease-stained dock workers seated on the barrels and boxes placed in a semicircle on the dock.

"The rules are simple and the same as always," yelled Sorley. "The fight is stopped when someone gets knocked down or is bleeding sufficiently to cause worry."

That last part, "sufficiently to cause worry," was Sorley's most recent addition to the fight agenda. He thought it made him look and sound like more of a gentleman.

"Pa, that kid's a big un." A nervous kind of fright was beginning to replace the guilt Michael Dowling had been feeling. But fear was more foreign than courage, and he stepped into the chalk-marked circle.

The big kid walked right up and

swung hard at Dowling's right arm. Mike
danced gingerly away, but Mannari's flying
fist had caught Dowling on the shirt. It
caused him to teeter slightly towards the
water's edge.

"Yeah, Tony Red... you 'bout got
him!" yelled a whiskey-thickened voice from
the rear.

Most of the bettors Sorley had rounded up had been talked into placing their
money on the Italian kid. The crowd,
smelling of grease and drink, liked a long
fight. But there was nothing wrong with
getting it over quickly, taking the money and
heading back to the saloon.

Thwapp! It wasn't a loud noise, but
everyone heard it. Mike Dowling had pivot-
ed from one foot to another each time getting
closer to his opponent. He faked a move to
Red's left side. As the big kid moved to
protect his left, Dowling literally jumped at
his right, fist extended, and popped the older
boy in the nose. The blood started squirting
immediately.

Sorley, for reasons no one could
explain nor bothered to contest, was also the

ref. He wanted nothing more than to end the fight and walk away with a hat full of money. But lynchings were still occasionally heard of along the Mississippi, and he allowed the fight to continue over the protests of the few betting on Dowling.

Tony Mannari was mad, he felt the immediate need to annihilate the younger boy and two-stepped toward him. The bigger kid wiped at his chin and a small stream of red became a large smear of blood. Then, in a move that looked more like wrestling, Mannari grabbed Dowling by the shirt. Swearing obscenities, he held him with his left hand while he smashed the younger boy in his stomach with three quick rights.

Dowling was hurt. He looked for help from the make-believe referee and stumbled backward, bent at the waist. The crowd hissed a reaction.

*He's mean, this one's a mean one.* Michael's thoughts crashed at him like spitting lightning. He could feel his racing, pounding pulse inside his brain. *Come on Mike, get your breath. You can get this guy! Get behind him, fake him!*

The smaller boy started a little dance step. His sore stomach screamed it's anger.

Mannari was ready to end this one. He moved towards Dowling in a deliberate fashion. He was slow and his intentions were easily read by the 11-year old.

Dowling was ready and he was quicker. As Tony swung hard, his target darted to his left then danced to his back. The redhead turned to face his opponent just as Dowling's fist caught him on the jaw. It wasn't enough to knock him down, but the uneven planks on the dock were.

Mannari staggered back, about to catch himself, when his right heel caught the rough wood and he collapsed quickly in a tangled pile.

His return to his feet was just as quick. But, it was all Sorley needed; a bloody nose and a fall. The fight was over.

Mannari tried but couldn't stop the tears that mingled with the dirt and blood on the front of his tattered shirt. The boy had been hurt. But the bloody nose was superficial compared to his crippled pride.

"I could have beat him, you know that. Give me another shot at the wimp. I tripped on the dock. You saw that, everyone saw that!"

He yelled at anyone who would listen, but most of the spectators had just lost money and felt little sympathy for the angry redhead.

"We got us a total of twenty-one dollars for that one Dowling. That makes fourteen for you and seven for me." It was a convenient figure, Sorley thought, as he placed a wad of worn bills into Dowling's hand. *Easily divided by three.*

"Whad' ya say Mikey? Can't be too down 'bout that can we?" The father squatted a bit so that he could whisper to his son. "Yuh know, most o' the men work days fer that. If they knew how much we be makin' in five minutes they'd be fer skinnin' us alive."

The younger Dowling smiled. He was proud. "Not bad Pa. I guess I could fight fer a long time, make a lot uv money, but mom would be feelin' bad." He looked down and kicked at a knothole in a wooden plank. "She wanted me ta git some schoolin', ta maybe be a priest or somethin'... to be somebody."

The young boy paused for a moment

in thought and then looked back up at his father. "And I guess I ain't bein' anythin' yet."

"Oh c'mon now, lad." John Dowling placed a rough paw on his son's shoulder. "C'mon, Mikey, it's gon' take some time, but ye kin do it. An' r'member whut yer mom always would say. She said she wanted fer yuh ta walk straight an' tall... to always walk straight an' tall. Do you r'member thet, Son?"

"Yeah, Pa, I 'member... straight and tall."

In New York's Hippodrome Michael Dowling continued, "I left St. Louis... took a boat up the river with my father. We somehow ended up in Chicago. Dad earned a little money doing carpentry work. He was very good at it. I sold flowers outside of McVicker's Theater. During that time I lived out near the rail yards with my Pa. Sometimes I gathered coal from along the tracks and sold it door to door."

"I remember passing many cold nights watching the rats march by. I always wondered where they were going, where they had come from. They seemed to have no plans, just wandering around."

Dowling paused for a moment, looked at a brunette woman in the audience, and started in again. "At 11-years-old I realized I was just like those dang rats, going nowhere, just wandering around."

"It was about that time that I bought my first English primer. I began reading about grammar. Then I bought a book on arithmetic. I carried those books around in a little canvas bag. I wore their pages right out."

The huge room was very quiet. Several soldiers leaned forward. The men were beginning to believe that, if nothing else, this Dowling was a decent storyteller.

The speaker had some difficulty relating what happened next. "My Dad, My Pa," he paused and nervously wiped at his forehead. "My Dad and I just kind of went our separate ways. Oh, he didn't just up and leave me, it wasn't like that. I just decided I might like to try things on my own."

He cleared his throat and looked around. "I saw my Dad briefly a few more times, but it was time to head out. I figured it would be tough. But I loved a challenge. Always have." A slight bead of sweat released itself from the furrows of Dowling's forehead and slid an inch toward his right eye. He wiped it away and continued.

"When I was on my own, the thought occurred to me that maybe I was becoming like one of those orphans on Sterling Street in St. Louis. I did everything possible to keep from becoming an orphan. I hauled water for awhile on a wheat farm. One day I read about there being some jobs out west on the Dakota Plains."

"I was glad I had learned to read. I loved to read newspapers. I found a little article that said there was real money in the cattle business in the Dakota territories. I had wanted to be a cowboy ever since one winter when I had been given the opportunity to attend some basic school classes in Chicago."

*It was an eerie concert of muffled cries that seemed to come from the outer reaches of hell. "Death masks," he thought.*

# CHAPTER TWO

On the Midwestern plains, seas of yellow grain turn September into gold. But it's the kind of gold that makes farmers nervous. It means the clock is ticking and a year's profit could be lost if the grain isn't harvested before the first snows end the season. Cattle ranchers, too, treat September with some anxiety. Steers, fat on the green grass of summer, must be taken to market before the winds of November come howling.

"You ain't worth a damn, Willards." Buck Willards, a cowhand at the Gunderson cattle ranch, had just emptied a round of six bullets on ten bottles and had scored one meager hit.

In the bright Indian summer sun, three men were passing the time at the edge of a large corral filled with nervous brown and white cows.

"And you think you're better?"

Charles Gunderson, a middle-aged man with a slow drawl and one of the owners of the Gunderson operation, knew he was better. "Yeah, I could beat that with an empty revolver." He turned to the third man. "How 'bout you Dowling, wanna try?"

Michael Dowling was 14 now. The handsome youth looked much older and was often given the work of a man.

"Yeah, I'll give it a go."

"Here, take my gun."

"Nope, don't need it." Dowling leaped off the fence and walked to a small white Indian pony named Charlie. It was his horse, partial pay for hauling hay the summer before. Mike fished in a pocket of a saddlebag and began to unravel a long leather whip. "How about you let me try this thing."

Gunderson exchanged looks with Willards, "That'll be all right... and Dowling, you get 10 tries to get five hits."

"I can do that." Dowling spoke with a

smooth self-confidence, uncharacteristic of a boy his age.

"If you can," said Gunderson, "I'm gonna make you a deal."

"What sort of deal?"

"A deal that'll make you rich," he chuckled.

In the three years since leaving Chicago, Michael Dowling had become very confident. He knew there were tasks that he was not equal to. But he sincerely believed they were rare. He had earned money to pay for more books and was learning history and science. He was teaching himself to speak and write a gentleman's brand of English.

"Crack-crash, crack-crash, crack-crash." The first three bottles exploded as the leather tongue snapped at them. "Hold it!" It was Buck Willards. "He's got 'em Charles. No sense breaking more bottles for nuthin'."

Charles Gunderson knew Dowling would more than likely break all the bottles. But he wanted the entertainment. "OK, you're right." Gunderson walked closer to Dowling and took the whip from the smiling kid. "Mike, that's a fine piece of equipment, but you'll need your pistol for what I want you to do. Here's the deal, and I know you can do it."

He whirled about on the worn heel of his boot and faced the herd of restless steers inside the wooden fence. "Those cows you been taking care of all summer, there're about five or six hundred, right?"

"There's five hundred and eighty five Mr. Gunderson." Dowling prided himself on keeping an accurate inventory of the herd.

"Well, those cows need to be at the railhead in Canby by the twentieth day of October. You get 'em there and you get an extra 25 cents a cow."

Dowling tried to be business-like, but he couldn't hold back. "That's a buck fifty, a dollar fifty per cow for the summer!" The arithmetic churning in his head was almost audible. The words shot from his lips like bullets from a gun slinger's hip. "That's what, seven, eight, nine hundred dollars, something like that!"

"You know I can do that. I'll leave in..." He paused to gather his composure and act the part of a man calculating something. But he knew exactly how long it would take to be ready, "I'll leave in ten days."

Then he spoke much slower, with as much authority as he could pull from his teenage being. "Those cows will be at the railhead in Canby by October twentieth... probably sooner. You got my word on that."

Charles Gunderson looked at Willards then looked back at Dowling. "Then it's as good as done. I'm riding into Canby with a wagon load of wheat. I'll see you there. And remember, Mike, you gotta keep 'em moving. Once you leave, you should be able to make eight, maybe ten miles each day."

Michael Dowling believed, among other things, that courtesy was as important as dependability. "Yes sir, Mr. Gunderson, you can count on that. I'll have all those cows in Canby long before October the twentieth."

Neither of them considered that there might be delays.

The plains west of Canby, Minnesota, look like the top of a loaf of homemade bread. From a distance they're gently rounded, from the curvature of the earth. But, if you're right on top of them, they are mostly flat, with occasional small rises, dips and gullies. There are trees, clumps of trees, but no one ever needed anything more sophisticated than one or two hands to count them on. Most of the groves were planted by farmers to protect their buildings from snow, wind and sun.

The prairie grass seems to move like a phantom army of slender soldiers, marching onward in a make-believe drill that rarely ends. Dowling was counting on the grass to keep five hundred and eighty-five hungry cows fed during their five day march.

The October sun played on the surface of the small creek that Dowling was now coaxing his cattle through. He knew it was normal to see two or three men herding this number of steers, but he loved a challenge, and he had little doubt he could pull this thing off by himself. Just the fact that Charles Gunderson had given him the job was sufficient reason for his self-confidence to swell. The warmth of the sun and the feeling of control gave way to a burst of optimistic thoughts.

*You're on your way, Michael Dowling. No orphanage for you. You're your own man, you don't need any parents.*

But he knew that was wrong.

He was providing for himself. The cattle business on the Dakota Plains had been all he had hoped for. He guessed he was earning more money in one summer than his father had ever earned in one year; although there was no way to confirm that. He felt a strange desire to try to prove it and wondered why.

But Dowling had come to a conclusion that felt dark and empty. He believed he would never see his father again and wondered why the thought had wedged into his mind. The really hard times came when he saw other boys his age with their families. He wondered what they did in their homes behind closed doors. Were there games and singing? What was it like?

*But it's OK, Mike.* His self-talk always provided comfort. *It's OK. Maybe*

*one day you'll marry and have a big old family
with a big house... a big ranch house... a cattle
operation!*

"Hey, hey now, get back there!" Mike
yelled at a small group of five or six of the
beasts that thought a right turn, and not a left,
was the appropriate thing on the opposite side
of the creek. Dowling forced a shrill whistle
from his lips, then called out to the far side of
the herd. "Yo, Silver, get on over here." He
thought it wise to solicit his dog's help in
bringing in the rebel cows.

Dowling would tell anyone who asked
the story of his dog. Silver was a stray that
just sort of ended up hanging around the
Pedersen Ranch about a year-and-a-half ago.
Mike hadn't paid much attention to him until
that morning in August when he and two men
found the dog crying in an awful way. His
left front paw was securely clamped into a
small silver animal trap. His face mirrored
something that perplexed Mike Dowling.

The older man in the group jumped
off his horse, inspected the leg of the dirty
mutt, walked back to his saddle and pulled an
aging rifle from a sling.

Injured animals were put out of their misery quickly.

Dowling realized what he was seeing in the eyes of the pathetic, injured dog. It wasn't fear or pain, but a dim sparkle that looked like courage and a will to continue his life. He didn't so much feel sorry for the mutt. It was more a kind of respect and awe.

The boy talked the older man out of using the bullet and within three weeks the dog was Dowling's closest companion. The name Silver came from the color of the trap.

Mike believed the dog had a rich heritage that probably included a collie and some kind of much smaller dog. The pup, with its curly brown fur and long snout, weighed about fifty pounds and ran with a pace that gave no hint of his cruel meeting with the steel trap. Curiously, there was a slight but noticeable limp when the dog walked. But when he ran, there were few of his kind that could keep up.

The dark clouds moving in behind the boy and his group of animals weren't noticeable at first. But by about 5 p.m. as Mike scurried about setting up the second night's camp, he was staring at them and wondering if those clouds might not mean snow. It was early in the season, but early snows were not unheard of. Besides, in the last hour the temperature must have dropped fifteen degrees. He had heard the horror stories of blizzards on the open prairies, but only smiled. Another way to prove myself.

*What's a little snow? We can handle it.*

The boy tended to Charlie, making sure the horse would be comfortable in the event it did snow, and then placed a bedroll for he and his dog on the ground. "Come on, Silver, get on over here. Might be some snow." He beckoned to the dog to lie between him and the diminishing flames of his small campfire. Both slept soundly until almost midnight.

Dowling heard the storm before he felt it. It wasn't the wind, it was cows.

They were bawling, making a sound he had not heard before. It was frightening.

His first thoughts were to pull his knees further into his chest and fall back asleep, head buried within the bedroll. He acted on the thought and closed his eyes, but now Silver was barking, and he knew he had to investigate before resuming his sleep.

For Michael Dowling there would be no more sleep on this night.

A wet awakening is uncomfortable, but adding the dimension of cold is to make things much worse. The temperature, twenty nine miles west of Canby, Minnesota, had dropped below freezing. The boy guessed it was in the mid twenties.

"Silver come here, come over here boy." Dowling struggled into warmer clothes. The nighttime air was angry with horizontal lines of ice and snow, ice knifing in from the west and it was piercing his face.

*Wouldn't you know it. An ice storm in October. I don't need this. I'm out to prove something here. I need to get these cows to Canby on time. Why me? Why now?*

Dowling's thoughts left a cold, bitter taste in his mouth. He knew he was concerned, maybe a little frightened, but he managed to push the thoughts into a dark hole. He contemplated his next move.

It was the sound of the cattle that broke his concentration. All around him was the sound of struggle. It wasn't the normal "mooing" and "grunting" he had become accustomed to during his two years on the range. It was an eerie concert of muffled cries that seemed to come from the outer reaches of hell. The cows, his cows were calling for help.

Lighting the oil lantern took some patience and skill. The sight of the yellow flame brought a slight feeling of comfort to the boy. "Let's go, Silver. Come on, let's go boy!" In the next instant he and his dog ran through the curtains of ice to the closest of the strange noises.

"Silver, it's suffocating, it can't breathe." The cow, lying on the ground, was jerking its head from side to side like the pendulum of some broken clock. Its face, its nose and mouth were covered with ice. The struggling animal was fighting to steal a breath of air in the terrifying, ice-clogged darkness.

Dowling only stared. Then a sudden surge of wind caused him to regain a sense of the danger. He looked into the darkness, listening keenly to the hundreds of crying animals. Then he started. "Come on, Silver, let's get the whip. Come on boy."

It was the butt of the whip he used as he ran tirelessly from cow to cow, clubbing them across the nose, breaking the masks of ice that were clogging the air passages. Death masks, he thought. "We can do it boy. Come on, Silver."

In the cloak of darkness Mike heard Charlie whinny and snort. "Was his horse OK?" "Could the pony survive?"

Dowling ran blindly through the deepening snow, the lantern had given out earlier. He charged against the angry wind using what he thought must certainly be a sixth sense.

The pony was fine, but there were cattle dying.

He raced back to the braying herd and darted among the mass of panic-stricken animals hitting them across the face with the cold butt of the soggy whip. At each stop the ice cracked into six or seven pieces and fell away. Each time it was almost the same; the freed animal roared with loud snorts as it gulped at the oxygen it had been denied.

Almost like a maniac, talking to

himself in demanding terms, Dowling stumbled to the next cow, then the next, sometimes seeing his target, sometimes only feeling.

*How many cows, Silver? How many have we freed? We've done more than a thousand... must've had to free-up some of them more than once. Tired, sore, hungry. But the snow is stopping. We're winning!*

At 5 a.m. the storm was giving up. For a moment he felt a brief hint of victory, but quickly dismissed it knowing there were still cows to check on. An hour later he ran through a group of cattle, surveying the herd, looking closely to see if any of them were still cloaked in the white masks. They all appeared to be free. But some of them were lying as if dead.

Charles Gunderson had arrived in Canby the evening of the storm. A restless night at one of the two boarding houses in town had been followed by a morning filled with tales of doom from the few cowboys who had arrived at the railhead.

His thoughts were beginning to be a whirlpool of numbers that meant mounting losses, diminished profits and a bleak winter. He could see a stretch of prairie littered with the corpses of bloating cows that belonged to him. And, what about the fate of the 14- year-old boy?

*What kind of fool would send a kid to deliver almost 600 cattle 55 miles away?*

He punished himself and walked into the mud of the town's main street.

At 7 a.m. the bodies of boy and dog were buried in the soggy bedroll. The sun had been up for almost an hour.

"Hey anybody alive in there, you OK?" It was a stranger's voice and he was kicking at the lifeless forms. Silver moved slightly, then bolted upright barking loudly, as if to cover his embarrassment for having been caught asleep.

Still no movement from the boy.

The cowhand was concerned. He stooped down and shook the body.

Dowling woke up. He reached into the

warm air and pulled down the rough blanket. He squinted into the morning sun at a tall figure staring down at him. "Good morning, how you doin'?"

Silver barked once more, this time at the stranger's horse.

There was snow on the ground, but it was forming small rivulets of muddy water and disappearing quickly. The sunshine was making a mockery of the lethal white stuff from the night before. The cattle stood looking at the two people. Silver shook his sides in an uncontrollable spasm as steam rose from his furry back. Charlie whinnied a salute to the growing day. The sun felt good.

The stranger spoke again. "Where're the rest of your crew? How'd you do in the storm?" He looked around him and adjusted his shoulders in a rolling motion. "Where're your men?" He was becoming very curious.

"Well, sir, there's my crew." Mike waved at his pony, then at Silver, who was seated now, watching the cattle.

"You alone?"

"Just my pony and dog."

"Well I'll be damned! My men are 'bout two miles away, lost 76 of our 800 cattle. Worse late summer ice storm I've ever seen."

Mike pulled himself from the wet bed roll and walked to his pony. The man reached into a large side pocket of his leather jacket and produced a brown bottle. A small square label proclaimed the contents to be Black Crow Whiskey. He removed the lid, placed the bottle to his mouth and cocked back his head in a quick jerk. He swallowed hard, wiped at his mouth with the back of his leather-like hand, and replaced the bottle's lid. He held the bottle toward the kid and slurred a question. "You want some of this stuff?"

Dowling considered the invitation a compliment, but politely declined.

"You know," the man slurred, "losing less than ten percent of a herd in a mess like that probably ain't bad." He belched quietly and continued. "How many did you lose?"

Dowling responded in a business-like manner. "I don't know. I reckon I lost some. I'll know in just a little bit."

The town of Canby, Minnesota, was neat rows of wooden houses, packed tightly against one another. They lined the muddy streets. The town looked like it had been built primarily to catch fire and burn to the ground. The stark contrast of the village against the empty prairie made it appear to be a government fort. There were no trees. The rail line ran along its edge from northwest to southeast.

At the railhead everyone was comparing stories, talking about their losses and, generally, trying to outdo the others' tales of bravado and adventure on the plains. The chaotic mix of animals, cowboys and rail agents seemed to be more exciting than ever to Dowling. Even the mud seemed to add to his feeling of well-being and pride.

This was the first time the teen had been in charge of a herd. He was bringing in the animals by himself. He sat in the saddle with unbridled pride as Charlie and Silver pushed the mob of bellowing cattle toward an empty corral.

Gunderson's pace was more rapid than normal as he moved from corral to corral. "You guys seen a herd out there with the Gunderson brand?"

"Nope, ain't seen nothin' like that. But you can be damned sure you're gonna have some losses."

It was only the 17th of October but Gunderson's anxiety was beginning to make a ticking sound in his gut. He jumped on the back of his horse and reined the animal back towards...

"Mr. Gunderson!" It was the voice of a young man calling from the far end of the gray, mud street.

Charles peered through slits of eyes toward the figure walking toward him.

*No, can't be. Dowling? Can't be!*

It was the barking dog that woke him from the momentary dream.

"Mike, you never looked so good. How'd things go? How are you? Are you OK?"

The cattle foreman seemed genuinely concerned about the boy as much as the cattle. "Everyone's coming in with a loss. It was a mean storm. How many'd we lose, do ya think?"

Mike knew the answer to that. "I don't know for sure," he fibbed a little, "we better count them."

Within twenty minutes the inventory had nearly ended. "Five, seventy five... five, seventy six... Mike!" Gunderson called out, "How'd you do it? You've only lost nine cows."

"Over here Mr. Gunderson, over here."

Dowling was pointing to nine more cows with the big 'G' little 'n' Gunderson brand. They somehow had found their way to a distant pen. "The other nine are over here!" He tried hard not to smile. He wanted to be serious and gruff like the other men, the seasoned veterans of the trail.

He failed. A huge smile spread over his face.

"Mr. Dowling, this is incredible." Gunderson had run to where the nine cows stood and was short of breath. "How did you do this?"

"Charlie and Silver, that's how we did it. They're about as good a crew as a cowboy could find." Dowling had already developed the habit of giving everyone but himself credit for accomplishment.

"I'm gonna give you those nine cows, in addition to your pay," exclaimed the excited ranch boss.

Michael Dowling had never felt more pride in his entire fourteen years. "Thank you sir, I appreciate that."

*School, that's where that extra money will go, more school, more books and more education.*

His thought was as natural as his smile.

*... and when the candidate slumbers, lady
death's kiss comes quickly without much
pain.*

# CHAPTER THREE

The house stood very close to the center of town, only about two blocks from the rail line. It was on the corner of Front and Haarfager Streets. A short picket fence surrounded a small yard that included the remnants of a few summer flowers. They were nothing more than clumps of brown with slight twists of mushy green stems. More than a few autumn frosts had come calling in early morning darkness and there were signs of the annual preparation for winter. Wood was stacked in a neat pile near the back door.

Michael Dowling, Silver and Charlie stood in the road looking at the home. The saddle on the horse included a large bag containing most of the boy's possessions.

The "room-for-rent" sign was intimidating to the 14-year-old. He needed a place to spend the winter, but this house was the kind he had fantasized about. It wasn't a grand mansion, but it was nice, and he guessed a nice family lived there.

He wondered if the family was rich and if he would qualify to live there. His saddlebag was filled with money; the proceeds from the sale of cattle and a summer of work. But, he didn't feel rich.

*Rich,* he thought, *meant a lot more money than I have. But I'm sure not poor. I'll be able to take care of myself at least until next summer when I'll make more money. I've got more than enough for that.*

He looked around to see if anyone was watching. He guessed the three of them might draw attention to themselves if they stood much longer near the dirt intersection, staring at the tidy house and yard.

"Should I ask 'em how much the room is?" He spoke quietly to the horse and dog.

"All right, I will." Michael tied his Indian pony to the fence, and with Silver scampering alongside, he pushed open the front gate, walked to the door and knocked.

A middle-aged woman opened the door almost immediately. He probably <u>was</u> being watched was his guess now. "Hello, son, what can I do for you?"

"Oh, well, ma'am, I was, I was just noticing your sign and was wondering if that room was still for rent." He was noticeably nervous.

"Yes, we have a room," Nellie Larson replied with a warm smile. "Are you with your folks?"

A soft blush of embarrassment rolled onto his face. "No, nope I'm all alone. I have a dog and a pony."

"What's your name, young man?" Nellie was beginning to be a little uneasy. There were many drifters who followed the farm work. But never had she met one this young.

"Who is it, Mom?" A blue-eyed, teenage girl came to the door, making Dowling even more uncomfortable. It was 16-year-old Sarah Larson, and her good looks told a story about sturdy Scandinavian ancestry.

"I'm not sure," was the mother's response.

"I'm sorry," came the reply. The boy removed his cap and felt a bead of sweat run down his back. "I'm Michael Dowling." He was eager to tell them about his accomplishment. "I just herded five hundred and eighty-five cows into the railhead." He looked at the ground, then at Silver. "I'm sorry, I don't have much of a family. My mother died when I was ten."

Michael began to look hard into this kind woman's eyes. "I don't know where my father is right now." He was anxious to tell her of his financial status. The words tumbled into the autumn air. "But I have money. I can pay whatever you're asking. I just want to spend the winter here and go to school and next summer get back into the cattle business."

Nellie was melting fast. "Well, Michael, we don't have anywhere to board your horse. But I think you and the dog can probably live here. The dog has to stay outside..."

Silver watched carefully as the woman spoke, his tail brushing the dust from the wooden porch. "...unless of course it's below zero. Then he can sleep by the stove in the corner of the kitchen."

"Thank you, Ma'am."

"It's Larson." She extended her hand. "You can call me Mrs. Larson, and this is Sarah."

"Mom, I think Michael can board his horse with the Leishmans over near Porter, out by Two-Mile Creek." Sarah was trying to be helpful. She always suspected that their new renter would be an older man who worked for the railroad. But this boy, she thought, was sixteen or seventeen and would be a welcome addition to their home.

James and Sarah Larson were fair people. They realized early that Mike Dowling was easily paying for board and room with the work he did. They told him to keep his weekly rent money.

Dowling was up early each morning to stoke the stove. He had already cleaned the sheds twice since October. With Christmas only three weeks away, he was helping Jim

Larson build a chest of drawers across town in a friend's barn. It was to be a present for Sarah. Dowling enjoyed the carpentry work. His father had taught him how to use a saw and hammer, and this project with Jim Larson was made even more enjoyable because the end result was going to a teenage girl. Michael Dowling was beginning to like the older girl. It didn't matter that he almost always felt uneasy in her presence. It was a good kind of uneasiness, and it made him feel warm.

Jim Larson was enjoying the pleasure of having a son.

"Mike, are you going to the church dinner with us tonight? It's that big Saturday night Christmas dinner they've been talking about for weeks. Are you going with us?" Larson was calling up the stairs to Dowling's small room in the attic. Mike, studying geometry in a fragile, worn book given him by his teacher at the Canby public school, quickly appeared at his door.

"I'm sorry, Mr. Larson, I've arranged for a ride on the Gunderson Lumber Wagon. A couple of men are going over towards

Porter. I've talked them into a ride so I can check on Charlie, my horse. I just want to make sure he's OK."

"You're not spending the night are you?"

"No, they're taking some lumber over and they'll be coming back later tonight. I'll be riding back with them."

"Be sure you stay warm. The skies look like snow."

"Thank you, sir, I will."


In the stale air of the Hippodrome, bodies shifted uneasily. They guessed they knew what was coming.

Dowling spoke with a small quiver in his voice. "That was the night that would change my life forever. I caught that ride with that farmer and his son. They had me and my dog seated in the back of the wagon with the lumber.

We pulled a large canvas over the top of us. Normally the ride from the Larson home to the little town of Porter, where Charlie was boarded, took about 30 or 40 minutes. But the snow was already very deep, and by the time the Gunderson's wagon came down the road to pick me up, I remember a few dried leaves on those bony, old elm trees were slowly twisting back and forth."

It's quiet on the plains of Minnesota. When it's cold, the quiet intensifies. It becomes a tangible thing that almost beckons one to grab a fistfull of sky and look it over closely. The jostling, jerking wagon with the farmer and his son in front and the boy and dog in the back was about the only sound to crease the still afternoon.

But, if you listened closely you could also hear a slight breeze blowing from the north.

There are various types of snow. The slush of a warm day is only a distant relative to the fine, icy dust that inhabits the air and ground when the temperature is told in single digits and minus signs. Even a faint breeze can become a master artist, brushing the white dust from field to road in a hypnotic display of long feather-like tendrils that writhe and wriggle in snake-like movements. Like cigarette smoke, the faint trails of snow hug the ground, gyrating and waltzing in an eerie, elusive fashion. And always, always the haunting moan that is the wind.

December 4th, 1880; the steady creaking of the wooden wagon and the occasional shifting of it's load of lumber, people and dog continued with the pale vocal accompaniment of the sinister wind. It seemed most people had stayed home. There was no other traffic on the isolated road in Yellow Medicine County.

On occasion the farmer, Joe Wright, commanded his two horses. "Hey giddup there! Come on now!" But, as if it was too cold, the Wright's sat in frozen silence as the horses attempted to find their way.

Fifteen minutes later the snow intensified and the wind picked up.


The human spirit is a positive thing and usually those who see a cloud on the horizon believe it will quietly pass and the sun will return. It's far easier to contemplate sunshine.

Up to now the wagon's driver had never even considered turning around. In his mind he was much closer to his destination than the security of those Canby houses behind him.    He pulled his collar up to his ears and squinted at the road ahead.    A stubborn, Norwegian mind told him that the wind wasn't much stronger than when they had left. The snow in the air was just about the same as a half-hour ago.

As he lied to himself he began to hear himself think about turning around.  But he knew he wouldn't.

There is an immeasurable quantity about a Minnesota blizzard that can be horribly frightening.  The wind and the cold are monsters.  But it's the wall that is most unnerving. Everywhere you look is a wall. A white wall, totally opaque.    Impenetrable. Immeasurable.

The heavy wall of white that drove head-on into the small wagon and its four occupants on that late afternoon tangled the mind and terrified the soul.    The same stubbornness that kept Joe Wright from turning around was now telling him that real men got through this kind of storm all the time. It would be tough, but he would make it.

But, the hard realization slowly smothered thoughts. The three human occupants on the ill-timed ride began to know that the attacking, frozen maelstrom was the kind of blizzard that would be talked about for years. The kind of storm that farmers dare not venture out to barns in, barns that are fifty feet from their houses, without a rope tied between their waists and their back-doors.

"Whoa, Silver, hold on!" The wagon hit a large bump and the entire load left the bed of the wagon in unison and fell back, six inches to the left of its origin.

Joe Wright screamed, "Gid back there! Hey you gid back there, Whoa!" The two horses were disoriented. The swirling snow blocked out everything that wasn't within an arm's length. The growing storm had erased everything, and the eyes of horses and men meant nothing.

"Hold on back there, Dowling, I don't think we're on the road anymore!" Michael understood now that the steady washboard bouncing of the wagon was because the horses were running through a field plowed in October. The furrows provided a corduroy ride that jarred and blurred the already poor vision.

Large flakes of snow blew into the flared nostrils of the crazed horses. They ran like insane creatures, tearing at their harnesses, trying to escape the frightening blindness.

"We can't see anything! I can't get these damned horses to stop!" The frantic voice of the man at the reins barely reached Dowlings ears. Mike's response was immediate. He clamped his right arm around the sideboard of the wagon and gripped his terrified dog with the other.

*A storm, all right. Could be a mean one,* thought Michael Dowling. *But we've been through these things before. And, Silver, what do you think... sometimes they're kind of fun!*

It was at first a relief to the boy when he and his dog were pitched from the maniac ride by a jarring bounce. The bone crashing had ended, and he and Silver were enveloped in a nest of cotton. He could hear Wright screaming at the horses as they were quickly consumed by the snarling white curtain. Then he could hear only the howl of the wind.

Then it was comical.

"Well, nice landing Silver," he laughed. There was no fear. He could do one of two things. One, he knew where the railroad track was. It was somewhere out there to the left. The dog and he could follow the steel lifelines back into town. Or, two, he could get back on the wagon and get into Porter and check on his horse. In an instant he determined that the second alternative was the best.

"Hey, get back here!" He and the dog began bounding like deer through the deep snow. They could see the wispish ruts left by the runaway wagon. "I fell off, hold on!" Dowling called against the yelling wind as he ran through the powdery drifts.

The reality of the situation hit him like a bucket of ice water. If he couldn't hear the wagon and the screaming of the hysterical driver, then it was a sure thing they couldn't hear him. His attempt to follow the tracks of the fugitive ride soon ended. They were no longer there. The parallel lines became nothing as the pelting flakes and ice erased all but their memory in a shroud of white.

"OK, Silver, let's go home." But Michael Dowling felt the first twinge of concern tickle his gut. It left a hollow, sick feeling. His mind conjured up pictures. *Cows... icemasks... suffocation...* He brushed at his face. "Come on boy." The sound of his voice was comforting to both.

He knew the railroad tracks were out here but, "Silver, it'd be a lot better if we could see. Come on boy I think they're in this direction. Let's go!" The dog skillfully used Dowling's deep footprints to hop after him, leaving no prints of his own.

The boy was sure, almost sure, that within 200 yards in their current direction they would be on the rails.

*No, not here. Maybe, maybe we back up and go 200 yards in the other direction. That's 400 yards, about a quarter of a mile.*

His mind raced in a tattletale direction, revealing a mounting fear. And there was something else, wasn't there? His feet hurt, they had been cold on the wagon, now they just hurt; a dull pain that hammered a slow beat.

It was the same in all directions. Nothing. No train tracks, no fence, no trees and no warmth. Only white nothingness and the constant sting of the frigid, howling menace that was the wind. And within a very short time the wind brought her partner along. Night. He came rushing down out of the somewhere sky, dressed in dark gray, and wrapped himself over the empty plains.

"All right Silver, there's got to be a farmhouse out here. We'll find a farmhouse. We can do that."

*You know we can do that. No one has to spend the night in the snow. There are houses all over the place. We'll find one. Need to. I've heard about temperatures going so low that the skin begins to freeze within two minutes. We'll find something... probably a warm farmhouse.*

But, he started to believe he might be

lying. He smiled. "Lying, why would I lie to myself. Come on Dowling you've been through these things before." *Just get out of the storm, get inside. You'll be OK.*

He squeezed his hands together in a tight fist and knocked them together as if applauding their new direction. The leather gloves were wet but still held a scant feeling of warmth.

*Clean hands..clean hands. I'll bet I have clean hands right now.*

The dreams- the thoughts of another time, and another place were welcome things and they slid easily into his mind.

*Clean hands! McVicker's theater in Chicago, I must have been about 11-years-old. It was about three years ago. Selling flowers, right there by the theater entrance... down to my last flowers. The man, he was a real gentleman, dressed very nice, with a love-ly lady.*

"Would you like those flowers my dear?" The man had seen the look in his partner's eye when she saw the small boy holding the flower arrangement.

"Oh yes, they're lovely," was her reply.

"Boy! Are those flowers for sale?" The man asked.

"Yes, yes, sir, I want to sell them!" The young Dowling was anxious to sell the last of his flowers so he could return to the shack he and his father shared near the rail yard.

"Let me see your hands!" The gentleman's voice was polished.

*Maybe he's an actor,* was Dowling's thought.

The boy held out his hands. They were spotless clean. He had always known that clean hands would help him to sell flowers.

"Would you like to pin the flowers on my lady?"

"Yeah, uh huh, I would."

The lady leaned down slightly while Michael pinned the flowers on her dress.

"Here, young man, here's a five dollar bill." Dowling didn't have the change for such a large sum.

"I'm sorry, sir," he was very apologetic, "Let me just run to the news stan', I can have the change for thet bill in jus' a moment."

"No, no, young man, it's all yours, it's all for you."

The man was closing Mike's fist around the five dollar bill. "Never mind the change. If you'll keep your hands clean, clean in every way, that's all I ask."

*I have, I've tried... I'll never forget that advice. Clean hands in every way...*

"MIKE, COME ON, MIKE YOU'RE LOST! YOU HAD BETTER FIND SOME-THING SOON." The self-talk, self-scream seemed to clear his head. The dog barked. Dowling was sure the temperature had dropped another ten degrees. The smell of wet wool from his scarf reminded him of the danger.

*Gotta keep dry, Mike, Gotta keep from getting too wet!*

Dowling brushed the snow from his shoulders and head. He squatted in the snow for a brief moment and rubbed the sides of his dog. Then he started walking again.

He guessed the snow was eighteen inches deep. It came to just below his knees. He wasn't sure if that was a foot and a half of new snow or if that was the total snow depth. Somewhere under the pool of the soft, white stuff there was probably a hard pack of previous snow. He wondered about it for a short time and then decided it didn't matter.

*Come on, Mike, you're looking for a house now; come on, you need to concentrate.*

His mind talked to him. He laughed, thinking it strange to be playing such mind games. *Old people must do this.*

"Silver, I've got something here, what's this?" Dowling had stumbled into something.

He reached down and found himself holding a piece of wood. There were more pieces. It was a woodpile. "We've got to be close. Come on boy, there is a house nearby. We've found the woodpile!"

He began to walk in the direction of

the home. *How do I know it's in this direction? Not so quick Dowling. Take it easy here!* His thoughts told him to retreat back to the pile of wood.

*Even a woodpile is better than nothing.*

He grabbed a piece of the frosted wood and hurled it into the white air. He heard nothing.

*These woodpiles are usually quite close to the house or barn. I know I'm going to hit something soon.*

The boy and the dog circled the pile, stopping occasionally so Michael could fling a chunk of the stuff in a slightly different direction.

*They were close now. It would only be moments before both of them would be inside the farmhouse of some kind people. He would be telling them about the last three or four hours in the storm... a little scared, but none the worse for the experience.*

They both listened against the cry of the gale for the warm thud that would announce something out there in the ivory darkness.

*But it wasn't really dark, was it?... Nighttime came, but what happened?*

The sun had set a long time ago, and yet it was still light. There was nothing to see, but it was light. White light was everywhere. The fierce, colorless vacuum of snow brought with it its own deceiving light, but it selfishly illuminated nothing more than itself, in the sub-zero air.

"Come on, Silver, let's grab a little wood. We'll move in this direction a bit. We'll find it." He was sure that within only moments the wood would hit the wooden wall of his fantasy farmhouse.

*Gotta be careful here. We don't want to break their window.*

He stopped to listen and chuckled at his last thought. But the cold silence froze the laugh, and it went nowhere.

Another plan. *We gotta do it. We'll*

*move away from the woodpile a little in each direction.*

The duo, like ghosts in an ethereal cloud bank, retreated  back to the pile of wood.   They moved thirty feet into the unknown, throwing wood and yelling for help. Then more wood and forty feet in another direction. Nothing.  Next, a fifty foot move, but still nothing.

It was only desperation that caused the pitiful spectacle to continue.   A boy and his dog trudging aimlessly, throwing here and there, helter-skelter  into the pale, gaping jaws of a fierce blizzard.  Never was there a response. No thud, no crack, only the monotonous, empty sound of the cruel wind that Michael Dowling hated in every way.

The 14-year-old knew he must be crying, but he couldn't be sure about tears. There was too much water on his face to really tell. He fought at the growing sense that they would spend the night in the snow. He had lost the woodpile. When he had attempted to return for more wood after a sixty foot foray for another toss at the make-believe house, the pile had disappeared. The white monster with the fierce howling voice and the stinging tongue had taken that from him too, and had only laughed with its frigid breath when he had uttered a simple, "please."

His toes and fingers were alternating between the sensation of sharp, burning stings and dull, hollow throbs. It was a cycle that soon dissolved into a blur of misery.

He didn't talk to the dog. He looked constantly to make sure Silver was nearby. But to talk, he thought, would almost be embarrassing. What would he say?

*Hey, Silver, I've got us through another one... What do you think, boy, looks like we made out again... I rescued you from that old trap just so you could limp along side me, walking to our grave... What do you think Silver?* Nope, there was only shame, and he knew it.

He wriggled ten stinging toes as he waded through the whitewashed emptiness that was everywhere. He brushed almost constantly at his face in a vain effort to see.

*My eyelids, my eyelashes they are*

*freezing shut. That's never happened. I wonder what I look like? Frozen eyelashes.*

And then he thought he heard the squeaking of the stupid, old lumber wagon. He stood still, held his breath and listened intently. A razor gust of wind only snickered back.

*Don't be an idiot Dowling! You're starting to hear things. Got to keep moving, got to keep walking. But where? Anywhere! Keep the wind to your back, Mike, don't walk into the wind!*

He was lost. He knew it mattered not in what direction they moved.

Like a tired machine the dwarf parade continued. And always there was snow in the air and on the ground. It swayed like a lethal white blade waiting to bring down anyone who would dare to oppose it.

A sudden thought. *How was Charlie? Was someone looking after his pony?* He wiped at what he now knew were tears. A running nose and weeping eyes had created a thick, painful, salty taste at the back of his throat. It only added to the gloom.

Then he felt something. "Wait a minute boy." The dog's bark was welcome against the cruel, growling wind.

"Wait boy, there's something here." Dowling felt a different sensation under his feet. There <u>was</u> something under them, but he didn't know what.

For a moment the thought of burrowing in the snow, trying to find something, was too much. He was too tired. He knew the temperature must be below zero, but he could only guess. Five below, maybe ten. The feeling in his fingers was a cruel mirage of mocking warmth. But yet there was some comfort in the counterfeit feeling, and he didn't want to disturb it with a digging frenzy.

*No, it's nothing. Let's keep walking.* But his mind turned on itself. *Come on, get on with it, Dowling. Something is down there, and it might save your life!*

He dug. Like a dog he clawed at the powder that hid the buried treasure. The ragged mutt, with a thousand tiny snow ornaments clinging to his fur, mimicked his owner's actions. Two figures, like centers in a colorless football game, hiked the snow, over and over to a nobody quarterback.

It was straw. Wet on top, but as they dug deeper, they found it to be dry. Somehow it seemed warm. Dowling knew this must be a hoax. Yet he had heard how farmer's hay-piles would occasionally start on fire by themselves.

*Spontaneous combustion they had called it.* He liked to repeat those words. *Spontaneous combustion. Hey, Mr. Gunderson, did you hear that Mr. Heinz had an incident of spontaneous combustion? It made him sound educated. What's the chance of our hay spontaneously combusting?*

"Come on, Dowling, your mind is wandering again." He spoke right out loud.

"Silver... we've found us a bed. Get down in there." And then a softer, quieter voice. "Thank you Lord."

The dog and boy burrowed in until

they reached the hard, frozen floor of the Minnesota Plain. They backed-off a foot and there, with about four feet of straw above them, they planned to spend the night. It was dry, soft and cold.

A brief hiss of the monster wind put a smile on Dowling's face. "We beat it, Silver, I think we beat it." The dog pushed himself closer, Michael pushed back. There was a feeling of peaceful relaxation. Dowling closed his eyes and wanted to sleep.

Frostbite and death from hypothermia are cunning things. They wait patiently, preparing their victims by introducing them to two clever deceptions: fatigue and peace. Both are facades- actors who entice the unwary into a lethal web. Drowsiness and a sense of well-being; and when the candidate slumbers, lady death's kiss comes quickly without much pain.

"STAY AWAKE OR YOU'LL DIE." Michael's yell startled the dog. It shifted in its position and immediately fell back to sleep. The boy envied the dog. He knew they could withstand much colder temperatures than humans. For a brief moment he was mad at Silver. But the emotion left as quickly as it had arrived and he began to take inventory of himself.

*The legs sting. They feel like a thousand, maybe a million ants are crawling over and inside of them. My left arm is tingly, the hand is numb. Right hand, it's a little better. Face feels hot and cold.*

He tried to rub at the coldest areas but it was difficult. Oftentimes, while sleeping on the plains during cattle drives, he had awakened to find an arm or a leg had "fallen asleep." The sensation now was similar.

The shivering was sporadic. He could lie feeling somewhat comfortable. Then, without warning, an icy wave would creep up his body like some frosty python, rivulating upward with it's slick, hideous skin.

The jerking, quivering convulsions that accompanied each cold flash kept him awake, and he thought them to be an annoying but well-meaning friend who tried to comfort in a clumsy and awkward way.

In the dark pocket that was their bed, Michael began to think of the hot days of summer.

*What about those times on the river with Pa, fighting with no shirt on. It was warm. The morning we were shooting bottles off the fence, the warm summer sun. The campfire. The hot cider last night at Larson's home. Swimming, yes swimming in the Mississippi. It was cold, but then you could lie in the warm sun, and slowly the sun would sink into your body, cradle you in its arms... you would get so hot you had to jump back in the river. The sun. It will never, ever be too hot for me again. I will never complain about heat for as long as I live.*

And then other thoughts.

*Is anybody looking for us? Are old Joe Wright and his kid safe? Does anyone know we're missing? Does anyone care? If I had a mother, would she care?*

The thoughts were cruel; he knew that. He was teasing himself in a rude fashion. But maybe it couldn't hurt. At least for a little while.

And now another sensation; warm eyelids. *Warm eyelids... and when I close them, they feel good, almost cool and soothing on red eyes.*

He smiled. He felt tired. The eyelids gently floated down. It felt good. He wondered what death was like.

*Maybe not bad. Maybe I'm dead now... or at least soon... it'll be all right. Maybe I'll see mom again. That would be nice, soooo nice...*

"COME ON DOWLING, YOU'RE NOT SLEEPING! STAY AWAKE OR YOU WILL DIE! "

Again the dog shifted in his sleep and Dowling pulled him closer to his side. He had a new determination to keep his eyes open in the icy darkness of the straw nest.

"This will not become my coffin," he breathed softly. "Please, dear Lord, help me."

The pain in his legs was leaving. There was hardly any pain now.

He couldn't feel anything.

*You LIARS!*

# CHAPTER FOUR

Like a pink pumpkin, the morning sun emerged from the misty white line that was the horizon. The skies were clear. The snow had stopped shortly after Michael and Silver had buried themselves in their straw bed. The dish of a sun was the only thing with even a hint of color. The plains, the trees, even the few surviving cattle surrounded by bleached fences, looked like hollow figures in a coloring book waiting for the touch of a wax crayon.

Michael Dowling guessed that morning had arrived hours ago. But, with limited strength, he wanted to make sure before he started digging out from the frozen mattress. "Come on, Silver, we've got work to do."

He was startled to hear that his speech sounded like a drunken slur. His face and lips felt numb and rubbery.

Like an old man, he began to slowly, tenderly push the straw to the side. It hurt. Each movement brought a dull pain to his bones and the feeling of hundreds of slender needles piercing his skin.

Slowly he wormed upward like a drunken ground hog intent upon learning of his shadow.

"Silver, hey pup, has anything ever looked so good?" They gazed at the pale disc of a sun hanging near the horizon. It offered no warmth, but its presence was somehow comforting.

Dowling clapped his hands together and was startled to hear a sound like blocks of wood. *Clean hands, keep your hands clean.* There was only the slightest feeling and it came from further up his arms.

The two heads, like tiny dots on a white map, slowly turned from side to side.

There it was.

"I knew it!" Michael stared at a small, yellow farmhouse about a half mile away. A thin thread of white smoke spiraled its way from a lonely stucco chimney into the ice-blue sky.

His first effort to pull himself to his feet ended in falling face first into the snow. The act of clearing the white powder from his eyes and mouth was observed by the dog, who wondered out loud, with a series of sharp barks, why his companion was so slow in getting underway.

Dowling tried to stand, but a pair of lifeless legs gave way. His feet were like two stones. He saw them, but his inner senses told him his body ended at his knees. His leather gloves had been lost hours before, devoured by the storm, and his hands looked white and rigid as if they were made of marble.

"We can make it, boy. Let's get to that house." The dog looked at the boy and tilted his head to one side. The boy's speech was somehow different.

The next events became distorted in the way a carnival's "house of mirrors" plays with images and illusions. The film of young Michael's life began playing in slow motion. He struggled to his hollow feet and then, with sharp pains in his upper legs, placed one foot in front of the other. He walked in a dream-like dimension. The feeling was like being on stilts, the major challenge being to keep his balance.     One cumbersome step after another, slowly progress came. Dowling kept his eyes on the farmhouse.

*Don't look down. The farmhouse, the one with the thread of smoke, it means a fire... warmth inside... I KNOW THAT HOUSE. It's Thor Landsvark's home. He and his wife know me. They'll be glad to see me!*

A half hour later the boy and the dog stared at a thermometer on the porch of the farmhouse.    It  was pinned at it's lowest reading: minus 50 degrees.  Dowling looked into the window but saw no one.   It didn't matter. There in a cast iron stove danced the golden flames of a fire.

He clenched both fists together and raised them to knock on the door. But for a fleeting moment something caught his eye. It was lying half buried in the  drifted snow not two feet from the bottom stair he had just awkwardly climbed.

*Strange*, he thought, *How come I didn't see that a moment ago?*

But he knew it had been there all along. It had been there all night. He recognized it almost instantly. It was a piece of wood, half-exposed by the unrelenting wind of the blizzard. It was one of the pieces he had thrown. The wood pile was there too, about 40 feet to the west. Scattered in all directions were the pieces of wood he had tossed in his futile effort to find shelter.

The door opened, Mary Landsvark stood in a rush of warm air that seemed almost hot. Michael feared he had frightened her. "Sorry, Mrs. Landsvark, I mean no harm. Can I come in for a little bit?" He spoke in the rubbery tones of a stroke victim.

The lady at the door stood motionless. Her face mirrored something that made Dowling uncomfortable. Her failure to speak created a hard lump inside Michael's belly.

*What is it? How bad do I look? What's so wrong?*

The boy standing on her front porch was a sick white. Not only his frost-covered clothing, but his face and hands too. They were bar-of-soap white. And they looked hard. They looked to be hard like soap. His left eye drooped and sagged as if something inside were broken.

Mrs. Landsvark and her husband, Thor, knew Michael Dowling. They had met at church and had heard reports of his work ethic and motivation.

"Well come in, Mike." She found the courage to speak. "You and your dog, please come in." She called to her husband, trying hard to remain calm. But Dowling could sense the woman's fear, and he wished he and Silver could just curl up by the warm stove and go to sleep.

"What is it Mary? Who is it? Well it's Mic..." Thor Landsvark entered the room and caught himself in midsentence. He, too, tried to hide the fright that grabbed him with a monster's hand. The picture of the boy pushed him beyond his abilities.

"Michael Dowling, you've gone and frozen yourself right up... yuh poor lad!"

"Mary, get two tubs of cold water. We need tuh try to get some circulation back into those limbs."

The wife ran for the tubs while the

startled man started rubbing Mike's hands and feet. Silver looked up with a hundred questions. The Landsvark's had scant medical knowledge, but most people in Minnesota knew what frostbite looked like, and they knew the customary methods of treatment.

In moments Mary returned with the tubs filled with cold water. Michael first coaxed his feet then his hands into the liquid. He sucked air into his lungs in a series of small rapid gasps.

"Mr. Landsvark," Dowling croaked, "this hurts much more than when they froze up." He was sure the water must be hot. His flesh burned in agony as if he had grasped a glowing branding iron.

"Michael, we gotta hope we can save them." Mary was entering the room with a cup of something hot.

*Save them?* He thought. *Of course... I might lose them! They cut them off, didn't they! A farmer... who was he? Someone near Granite Falls, he had a missing finger. Someone said they had to cut it off the winter he went after his lost cows.*

He was panting now as he sat looking down into the water. The cold liquid had formed ice casts around his hands. Mary Landsvark, still trying in vain not to show her fright, rubbed the ice away. "We'll get you back to the Larsons."

Thor placed a farm-weathered hand on Dowling's shoulder, "We'll get Doctor Farnsworth."


Marshall was a progressive town on the rail line about 30 miles southeast of Canby. The town boasted two doctors and one drugstore.

Gilbertson's drugstore was closed on Sunday, but Dr. J.W. Andrews, the medical authority for three counties, had an emergency, and Will Gilbertson had opened the store.

"Will, how much chloroform do you have?" Dr. Andrews, 55-years-old and clothed in a thick leather coat with a fur lining wore a weary look as he anticipated a wagon journey that would take all afternoon.

Dr. Farnsworth had sent the message last night: "Compound amputations are necessary to save his life. Even then, we have only a slight chance. Would like to perform the surgery Monday, December 20th. The boy is too weak to be moved to Marshall. Can you be here on Monday?"

Medicine on the prairie was a demanding thing. Patients rarely came to you. Travel was a time-consuming fact of life. Andrews had sent his affirmative response to Canby by way of a mail carrier the same afternoon.

"How much chloroform you going to need doctor?" Gilbertson knew that chloroform and ether meant "putting someone out."

"We'll probably need enough to keep a young lad out for three or four hours."

The drugstore owner knew better than to ask too many questions. He nervously shuffled through a shelf of brown, blue and clear bottles. "Looks like just one, and it's only about three-quarters full."

"I'll take it." Andrews searched the shelf with his eyes. "How about ether, do you have ether?"

Will Gilbertson rummaged on a second shelf. "One bottle of ether."

"I'll take that, too."

Will began to write something on a small pad of paper. The doctor stepped to the window, wiped away the frost and looked at the white landscape. "Some boy up in Canby got caught in that blizzard a few weeks ago. He's got serious gangrene in two legs, an arm and a hand. Doctor Farnsworth, up there, doesn't think he'll survive. I'm going up this afternoon. I've asked Doctor Little to go with me."

Gilbertson's face showed his concern. "You'll need more than these two bottles to keep him out for three or four hours."

Andrews turned back to face the druggist as he was wrapping the bottles in newspaper. "I know, I hope Doctor Andrews has some."

Dowling had told the story before. He knew there would be tears amongst his listeners. It was usually always the women. But tonight, in the Hippodrome, grown men had reached for handkerchiefs. On the front row a man with a hook for a right hand was clumsily wiping his eyes with a sleeve.

The same thoughts were entering the minds of many of the soldiers seated up front. *Is this why I came tonight, to vicariously live my own personal agony again through this man? Do I need to hear this?*

Somewhere about 30 rows back, a man stood up, inched his way to an aisle and left the room. No one on the front rows departed. All eyes remained on Michael Dowling. A soft look of respect was erasing the skepticism of a half-hour ago.

Dowling's voice was soft as he continued. "The two weeks after the blizzard, before the surgery, are hard for me to remember. I was very sick. I didn't eat much, I slept most of the time. Dr. Farnsworth, in Canby, massaged my legs and arms. I somehow believed everything was going to end all right."

"I placed a lot of faith in that doctor. I was only 14. I somehow knew he was doing the right the thing. I believed I would be walking out of that house by Christmas and I would be like every other teenage boy."

"Then he told me he was going to have to cut off my arm and legs."

"When I saw the tear in his eye, I knew he was serious. I became sicker than ever. I wanted to die."

Dowling hesitated, looked up at the ceiling and then returned the stare of a man seated in a wheelchair. "Some of you here know what a bone saw is. It's used to carve up beef." He looked away and swallowed. "Sometimes they are used for amputations."

"In order to save my life, the doctor told me I would have to have all the gangrenous tissue removed. He told me the amputations would take place in the Larson's home where I was renting that little attic room. He said something about Sarah, their daughter, being sent away for the day, to be with friends."

The room was too cheerful for the event that was about to take place. A coat of bright pink paint was the latest layer. Small drawings of peaceful scenes filled painted wooden frames that had been attached to the walls. A yellow flame burned in a black stove. Three oil lanterns produced a fine black smoke. A rag doll with a huge smile on its cloth face sat on a small shelf. Red flower curtains hung at the windows trying to mask the ice on the outside.

Christmas was only five days away, and streamers of red and green paper were draped high on the walls near the ceiling.

A large red and white, wooden Santa Claus stood on a window sill, grinning at a blue bottle of chloroform. A brass wind-up clock said 8:03 a.m.

Dr. Andrews spoke with Jim Larson in a hushed voice. "There is no other way. Both legs beneath the knee, the left arm below the elbow, and it looks like the fingers and half of the thumb on the right hand."

On the table, lying on an oilcloth was Michael John Dowling . He was six weeks shy of his fifteenth birthday. Doctor Little, true to his name- a small man, held a rag to the boy's nose. "I think he's ready," came his stern assessment. He was a young doctor, but already knew too much about life and death and bleeding. Dr. Farnsworth looked at Dr. Andrews. They nodded simultaneously.

A basket at the foot of the table was filled with strips of cloth; the remnants of pillow slips and sheets donated by neighbors.

"All right then." Dr. Andrews moved

to the table and pushed his fingers into Dowling's flesh near his left elbow. He probed, feeling for bones and tendons. "Right here, then; we'll make the first cut here." The surgery began.

In an adjoining room, next to a small decorated Christmas tree, Jim and Nellie Larson played at a pretense of reading from the family Bible. It was in vain. The rasping sound of the saw and the muffled voices were far too easy to hear. At one time Michael's voice brought them to their feet, but they thought better of looking into their kitchen.

Dr. Little held more chloroform to the young man's nose. A pile of bright red cloth strips was growing into a small mountain in a nearby tub. Needles, thread and tourniquets spilled from the table to the wooden floor.

At ten minutes past noon, the anesthesia was wearing off again. Dr. Farnsworth had contributed one full bottle of ether; but after four hours, all three bottles had been emptied and the bone saw had only begun it's hacking move through Mike

Dowling's left leg- the final amputation. Dr. Farnsworth yelled into the living room. His faltering voice told of his grave concern.

"Jim, go get some neighbors. We're going to need some help here!"

Larson, feeling dizzy, raced into the street. He stopped suddenly, steadying himself on a pile of snow. He thought he was going to vomit, but he didn't. It was only eight or ten minutes before he returned with P.A. Larson, Pete Jacobsen and William Miller.

The newcomers stopped in the doorway of the kitchen, mouths open, as they surveyed the gruesome picture in the dimly lit room.

"Come on now men we've got some work to do here." Doctor Farnsworth began yelling instructions. "He's waking up. Hold him down. Hold him tight or we'll never finish!"

The doctor wanted to speak. He knew what the others were thinking, but he gave no voice to the thoughts. He allowed their torment to stay burning within his throbbing head.

*A damned waste of time here, and it's a pity; he's such a strong boy. But a horse couldn't sustain this kind of blood loss. There is no way he can live. The mortician will have to be called. Damn it! What can I do. What can we do? Butchers! Is that what we are? Is that what we've become?*

Men at the rail terminal that Monday morning heard the screams, swallowed hard and looked away. They knew what was happening.

Nellie Larson fled the rear of her house, dodging ice and snow. Her route was a maze of unsteady turns that always brought her to within hearing distance of her home. Only long after the screaming stopped did she return.

The bleeding continued after the cutting and stitching had ceased. The three doctors hovered close to the boy, always applying more bandages, and tightening then loosening another tourniquet. The three neighbor men had returned to their homes at the earliest possible moment.

Doctor Farnsworth turned to a gray-faced Jim Larson who had entered the room. He whispered something as if he were in the presence of the dead. Larson whispered back. The doctor's next comment was in a slightly louder voice, but still not much more than a whisper. "He can never survive such an operation."

"You LIARS!"

Everyone in the room was stunned to see Dowling was coherent and moving his head from side to side. "You liars, I'll live longer than any of you."

Doctor Andrews quickly walked to the side of the boy. Placing a hand on his forehead he spoke softly. "Michael you need to rest. We'll move you into the bedroom. One of us will be here with you throughout the night. You must drink and you must rest, you've lost..." he hesitated, glanced quickly at Jim Larson then back. "You've lost a tremendous amount of blood."

Dowling either fell back asleep or slipped into unconsciousness. Doctor Farnsworth felt for a pulse. It was there, but it was very weak.

Doctor Little had wrapped the amputated limbs in a white sheet to be buried.

February 17th presented itself with no sky. The day had more of a grayish-white ceiling that squashed any hopes of sunshine. Winter continued in the small town of Canby.

All but the smallest baby had learned about Michael Dowling. The story of his night in the blizzard and the awful consequence had spread to most of the nearby counties. Somehow the boy had survived the operation. Most people believed it was an act of God and wondered why.

In the Larson kitchen, Nellie labored near the stove. It wasn't easy, but she tried mightily to construct a cake for Michael Dowling. It was his fifteenth birthday. Six weeks had passed since the day he had lost half of his body.

The young man's life had become a series of fitful naps. Sleep, dreams, nightmares, sweats, and upon each reawakening the awful sickness that came from the realization that he had been cut in half.

He dreamed he was a prisoner inside a body that would not move, could not move.

He struggled to remain asleep. To awaken meant the end of the dream and the beginning of the nightmare. It meant real life, his life, and he believed there wasn't much left of it.

Dowling's spirits plunged to an all time low. He wanted to see no one. He wallowed in his thoughts.

*Why has the whole foundation of my life been pulled out from under me? Life has given me a raw deal! Why was I so stupid to pray to stay alive?. Why was I so strong to survive only to become this thing, this piece of flesh?*

"Happy Birthday, Michael." Sarah Larson attempted a smile. "It was fifteen years ago today you were born in Huntington, Massachusetts." Both she and Dowling knew talk was difficult. Always her eyes drifted to the bandages that marked the end of Michael's legs and arm. She tried but felt betrayed by her quivering voice and nervous smile.

"Do you want to play cards?" Sarah wanted desperately to entertain the boy on his birthday. "OK," was the reply from Dowling.

He was propped up in a large wooden chair, a blanket across his lap. His eyes looked anywhere but at Sarah. His distorted speech had improved. The rubbery tones had disappeared.

The young lady placed the sick boy's cards between the closed pages of the family Bible. Michael pointed to the cards he wanted played. There was little life to the game and it quickly died.

And then there was a brief sparkle in Michael's eyes. A ragged, brown dog had entered the room. It raced to Dowling's side, uncontrollably wagging its gnarled tail. Then with a mighty leap it fell into his companion's lap, licking at the boy's smiling face. Michael patted the dog on the head with his bandaged right hand.

In the living room three girls from the neighborhood played the piano and sang songs. Dowling forced an occasional smile and thanked them for coming. The songs continued.

During a break between numbers, Michael could hear the muffled voices of the young ladies. "That poor boy, isn't it dreadful... he'll be helpless his whole life! He'll have to be dressed and even fed by other people."

Sarah pulled herself up from her place on the floor near Dowling's chair. She wanted desperately to silence the girls. She wasn't quick enough.

"You know, it's probably too bad he didn't die. It would have been much better for everyone."

There was a silence then. Michael could feel tears filling his eyes. He tried to wipe them away but couldn't. His emotions, churning in a whirlpool of anger, finally boiled over.

"I hate pity. I won't be like that. I want to be like everyone else! I won't be put on a shelf somewhere."

The pain of his physical predicament was now amplified by the embarrassment of uncontrollable crying. The barrage of tear-stained words continued. "It, it won't be like that. I... it will take some time, but don't throw me away! Don't do that! I'll be OK! You'll see!"

Outside a black plume of a cloud had settled over the town of Canby. A gust of wind threw a handful of sleet against the kitchen window.

The birthday party on Haarfager Street was over.

*There was a damp and cold silence in the courtroom. He felt chills and remembered the night that had necessitated this meeting.*

# CHAPTER FIVE

There is something about anticipation. It seems the longer you wait for something, the more you expect from the event waited for. On the northern plains people wait a long time for the arrival of spring. Rarely is their anticipation unrewarded. Spring in Minnesota may not be better than other parts of the country, but people there will tell you differently. It's probably because the wait is so long.

When the warm rays of sunshine coax the first tulips, crocuses and daffodils from their slumber, everything seems good. When a new dress of green grass replaces the prairie's old brown winter suit, everyone's future improves.

The boy in the attic room was feeling a warm spark of optimism. It had been months since he had felt good; but now, with the arrival of spring something was happening inside of Dowling's head.

And now he had a plan.

He hadn't thought it strange at all. It was about the third or fourth day of really good spring weather when he made a bold announcement. He had been placed in the chair where he spent most of his waking hours. He had already been dressed by Jim Larson. Dowling easily preferred the male member of the house dressing him. It was much too embarrassing, for the 15-year-old to be dressed by Mrs. Larson.

It was noticeable to everyone in the home that the boy was doing as much as he could for himself. He appeared to take great pleasure in combing his own hair with a tortoise shell comb Sarah had given him for his birthday. It was a time consuming process, but he was mastering the art of wrapping the stubs of his remaining right hand around various objects. His right arm was becoming quite strong. In fact, he often fantasized about exercising that arm until he had a "two foot" bicep.

Dowling, with a slight "bounce," shifted himself in his chair. He moved the deformed hand through his freshly combed hair and nervously cleared his throat.

"Mr. and Mrs. Larson, it's time for me to be moving on. I thank you for everything you've done. You have been my family when I had none. I will always be indebted to you. Thank you, but it's time for me to be moving on."

Both Larsons felt a certain pity for the boy, and now they thought he was delirious. Nellie's face was white. It was James Larson who finally found something to say.

"But Michael, what are you going to do? How, uh... how are you going to do it?"

Mike felt the opportunity to talk again about his success as a cattle driver and started in with enthusiasm.

"Well, you know I had almost a thousand dollars when I got here last fall." He looked down and then back into the kind eyes of Jim Larson. "Well... most of that is gone now. I know people in town have contributed money and the doctors gave me most of their services. But still, most of that money went to additional costs, and..."

Nellie Larson reached out to touch his hand and interrupted him. "Mike, you will be taken care of here. You don't have to worry a thing about money. We can take care of you." The Larsons genuinely loved the boy who had come to live with them.

Michael felt the warmth of this lady's love and blushed slightly. "I know, I thank you for that. But, well... I'm 15-years-old now, and I need to start thinking about college and how to earn a living and things like that. I'm thinkin' I'd like to move to Granite Falls and get me some kind of a job. I can paint fences, I can maybe sell magazine or newspaper subscriptions on a street corner. I'll find something. Most important, I want to get into high school there in the fall."

He looked at the floor and then began rubbing the stump of a thumb against the palm of his only hand. He looked back up at the two people who had been his parents for six months. "My mother always wanted me to be something and so I'm going to try real hard. She, uh... "

He looked away and tried to chuckle, but it didn't sound sincere. "She always wanted me to walk straight and tall. That will be a little harder now, but I'm gonna try."

Nellie desperately wanted to be of some help. "Would you like us to care for your dog?"

"Oh, would you? And then I could come back and visit Silver, maybe take him with me when I can." The boy was genuinely happy with the offer.

The Larsons nodded their heads in approval and wondered what this man of a boy would do next.


No one knows for sure why the Swedes, Norwegians, Germans and Irish settled in Minnesota. There's plenty of speculation. "Cold, it's the cold weather," some guess. Others believe the checkerboard of lakes and rivers reminded the new settlers of their homes, and furthermore, those same immigrants learned that the black, glacial soil would support potatoes.

Henry Bordewich, a stern Scandinavian with blonde hair and an iron jaw, had arrived in America from the Lofoten Islands, off the coast of Norway. He immediately volunteered to serve in the Civil War, then, with his wife, settled in Yellow Medicine County where he worked in the county courthouse.

They had three attractive daughters. Henry claimed his oldest daughter, Jennie, according to county records, was the first white girl born in the county.

"Jennie, come in here." Bordewich called to his child. A young girl with brunette hair entered the room. "Jennie, sit down."

"What is it father?"

"It's Michael Dowling."

"Oh, Mike," Jennie exclaimed. "What about him?"

Bordewich forced a stiff smile and continued in his "up and down" Norwegian cadence. "He's asked for my help."

"He's going before the county commission next week and he wants me to try my influence with Mr. Dahley and Mr. Stoltenberg. He's guessin' that because they're Norwegians, too, I could help him out."

"Could you? Nobody tries harder than Mike. In the two years he's been here staying with Ole Lende he's worked very hard. Just last week he was pulling himself around on the ground painting the fence at the court house. Did you see him, Papa?"

"I did see him. I did see the lad. It was almost a sad sight. If it wasn't for that big smile of his, I would have felt sorry for him. But somehow I don't pity the boy, I just wish... hope I can help him. Everyone wants to help him."

"He's a handsome one, isn't he, Papa? I mean if he wasn't just a stub of a guy, I think I could like him."

The father's reply was almost stern. "Jennie, you're much too young to be thinking about boys." He paused and contradicted himself. "I just wanted to know what you thought of him. He's done a fine bit of work for me in the office. He's got very good penmanship for having only half a hand."

"Mike's six years older than me, Father, but I still like him. You watch him. He's going to be an important man one day."

"Oh, you think so?" He made a sweeping motion with his hand. "Now get out of here, run along. I have work to do now, go on."

Henry Bordewich walked to the window of the living room in the small frame home not more than two blocks from the courthouse; the official center of Granite Falls. He placed his hands on the wooden windowsill and leaned forward, surveying the scene. His daughter was running out of the yard to join two other girls.

*Only 11-years-old and she's already thinking about boys.* This was new for Bordewich. After all, Jennie was his oldest. It was an uneasy thing, and he wondered why he was giving it much thought.

*There'll be time enough for that kind of stuff later. She's only 11.*

And then a thought cut into his mind. Its arrival almost left a slight pain over his right eye. He rubbed at his forehead.

*What if Jennie were to begin hanging around someone like Dowling; a cripple. She's much too good for him. She deserves a whole man. She'll be raised a smart, educated, cultured woman. What if she were to marry someone like Michael Dowling? It would ruin her whole life, wouldn't it?*

A group of farm boys pushing a baby buggy down a wagon-rutted street with a teenage boy inside, would be just cause for a second look in most midwestern towns. In fact, it would look strange anywhere. In Granite Falls the scene had become quite ordinary. For two years, teenaged boys and some girls had jockeyed for their turn at wheeling the legless Dowling to school.

Mike had learned early to accept the ride. There were no other options. The arrangement had worked well. He had made friends with almost everyone. But Dowling wondered if he would ever really fit in. He never played ball with them, never danced with the girls and never took a summertime swim in the lakes and ponds that were scattered in all directions.

But Michael Dowling had proved he could learn. He had done well in high school and now he believed he was ready for college. In his active mind, it was the next logical step.

Only one obstacle dimmed the picture of his future: he was a public charge. The county paid his way. He had little money for himself. He was at the mercy of the county government, and he knew it.

"Absolutely beautiful day isn't it, Michael?" Jennie Bordewich was walking with an entourage of three boys escorting Dowling to the county courthouse. She was slightly out of breath as the group passed a blossoming apple tree.

"It's OK, Jennie, it's not bad."

Dowling was sick inside. He knew the outcome of this meeting might crush his plans and dreams. It might kill him.

At the steps of the Yellow Medicine County Courthouse, the boys brought the baby carriage to a halt.

"Thanks," Michael spoke. "I'll repay you sometime." They somehow believed he meant it.

"Well, how're we gonna get me in there?" Michael sounded somber, but then followed the question with a tiny smile.

With a strong right arm, Dowling centered himself on a small board at the bottom of the canvas vehicle. The three boys and one girl each grabbed an end of the crude seat and, one step at a time, inched their way up the weather-pitted, concrete steps of the courthouse.

As the group entered the wood-paneled, commission chambers, an uneasy quiet replaced the drone of voices and shuffling papers. The three somber-faced commissioners sat in front of a yellowed American flag draped across the wall.

On one end sat Ole J. Dahly, one of the Norwegians. He was balding and wore small glasses that seemed to amplify a pair of pale, gray eyes. He had the habit of moving his head in a slight up and down motion just before he began speaking.

On the other end was Theodore Stoltenberg, a large immigrant from Norway who had waves of white hair tarnished only slightly with a hint of blonde from earlier years.

In the middle was the 70-year-old chairman, S.A. Hall, a New Englander. He was a more educated man than his two associates, and his speech and manner reflected it. His appearance somehow seemed to be dominated by a black, leather coat that bore a resemblance of having once fit him.

"Mr. Dowling." It was the chairman. "Nice of you to come to see us. Please have a seat... uh, uh you may rest over there." He was a bit flustered over what he perceived to be a glaring error in social graces and quickly glanced around to see how many observers may have witnessed the blunder.

Michael was placed on a pew-type bench. The three boys left the room, and Jennie walked to the rear and sat down.

"Now what is it we can do for you?" His question was delivered with some apprehension. The men had known about this meeting since the day, one week ago, when Henry Bordewich had left a note with the county clerk. The three had openly questioned each other about Dowling's motives. They were a bit uneasy and had deliberated over the matter for a full morning. They had come to a conclusion and believed they were prepared.

"Mr. Chairman," Dowling knew Hall was the one who wielded the most influence, but he was betting that his friend, Bordewich, had been influential on the Norwegians.

"I'm here to ask for a little help. I know I can repay any kindness you can..."

"Mr. Dowling." It was the chairman again. "We have contacted a family in the area, and we are pleased to inform you that we have appropriated two dollars a week to pay the family to take care of you."

Mr. Dahly finished the thought with his head bobbing. "For as long as is necessary. Even the rest of your life, if needs be."

The other Norwegian enthusiastically added his approval to the plan. "Yah, that's right!"

Michael shifted his half body and looked at Jennie at the rear of the room. She was biting her lip and quickly glanced away. Michael swung back to the commissioners and wiped at his eye. He felt the moisture there and it made him angry.

*A fight*, he thought to himself. *This is going to be a fight, and I think I can win. I have a future. These men can't rob me of that. I don't want to be pushed around like a baby for the rest of my life.*

He looked down at his deformed hand. He rubbed it on his stomach and thought about what to say next. But Stoltenberg spoke first.

"Yah, well let's not be so fast here. Michael, what duh you think?"

"Mr. Stoltenberg, I was thinking..." he struggled to hide his humiliation. "I was thinking that maybe if you men could give me just a year at Carleton College, over in Northfield, and help me get a pair of artificial legs, then if you can do that, I will repay you and I will never cost this county another cent for as long as I live."

The chairman stood up. Dowling felt a sudden urge to stand up with him. But he knew he couldn't. An icy wind slapped at the back of his neck.

Hall's voice was loud. He was irritated. "You can't back that up! You're just saying that. You have nothing to go on. We can't be putting money into something like that. Besides what are you going to do with just one year of college? One year of college, even at a fine school like Carleton won't do you hardly any good at all."

It seemed to Dowling that Hall was

beginning to consider the notion of schooling and he felt some encouragement.

"I, I can do it. I'll work two, three times as hard as the other students. I just need the chance."

Commissioner Stoltenberg spoke next in a slow drawl. "That would be a lot of money, Michael. Yah know we want to see you through this awful thing, but we need to be realistic."

"I mean it. I can do it. I know I can." Michael spoke with both anger and confidence. He looked out the window and then back, this time at the chairman. "I just need someone to believe in me, to give me a chance."

There was a long uncomfortable silence. Then the chairman spoke. "Michael, if you will excuse us, I'd like to talk with the other commissioners for a moment. We'll be right back. You stay right..." another verbal miscue and he knew it. "We'll be back in just a moment."

There was a damp and cold silence in the courtroom. Michael turned to look at Jennie only one time during the 15-minute wait. He felt chills and remembered the night that had necessitated this meeting.

*Cold, cold in here. Lonely. I need someone, one of those three men to be my friend. If they'll help, I'll spend my lifetime helping people. I'll somehow repay... I'll do it... I can do it! I know I can do it! But they don't think I can. How can I convince them? Someone help me!*

It was a prayer as much as anything.

Behind closed doors came the muffled voices of the commissioners. The volume rose then fell away again. The conversation apparently was intense.

*This is it,* thought Dowling, *I can't herd cattle. I can't do much of anything. I won't sit on a street corner much longer. I won't sell pencils in a cup. I can go to college, learn how to study, get an education. I can do that and then,* his thoughts raced, *and then anything is possible. I can be an accountant. Don't need legs for that just a brain. I can own something, be a businessman, own a bank. If they won't help me, I'll go to St. Paul... the White House...*

The door to the commission chambers opened. The three men with somber faces approached, shoes clacking on the wooden floor.

"Michael." He felt as vulnerable as that night in the blizzard. The three stood towering over him. He felt overpowered and terribly alone.

One of the Norwegians, Mr. Dahly, squatted to reach Dowling's eye level. He spoke again. "We've voted, and I must tell yuh the results. We voted two to one that we appropriate the funds to send yuh to Carleton. But, not for one year... only fer two terms. After that yu'll be on yer own."

Dowling scanned the faces of the three. *Who voted against me?* He was sure it was the chairman. *No, maybe not!* The chairman was smiling and so his guessing game had hit a snag.

*Maybe it was one of the Norwegians, maybe it was... It doesn't matter.*

The chairman, Mr. Hall, spoke next.

"We will get you the artificial legs. There is a place in Minneapolis. You'll get them."

The next voice was unexpected. "You won't be sorry. He'll do what he says. He means it! He can do anything!" It was Jennie Bordewich at the rear of the courtroom. She started running to be by Michael's side.

Dowling felt a bright, warm wave splash into his stomach. *It's done; I'm on my way! Life is good. No one will stop me now!*

"It shouldn't have mattered to me. I got my legs and the two terms at the college, but I continued to wonder who voted against me. It might have been the guy with the glasses. He probably needed some new ones. He had a real difficulty, I think, seeing past my minor disabilities."

In the Hippodrome the temperature was rising on the spring afternoon. Five thousand and six hundred bodies were radiating heat. Windows along the top of the building had been pushed open with long poles. An early season warmth, mixed with a blue-gray veil of cigarette smoke, was settling over the crowd.

Dowling took out a handkerchief with

the hook of his left hand and dabbed at his forehead. "It seems there are some people who need their vision corrected so they can see the real people, not just the little problems some of us have." Several men on the front rows clapped their appreciation for the remark. Others joined in. Dowling hadn't expected the applause and shuffled from one artificial foot to another. He spoke again.

"Now, it seems to me I'm about the only one standing in here. I've been speaking..." he pulled a watch from his breast pocket, "I've been speaking for about 45 minutes and none of you boys here in the front have offered me your chair."

There was laughter from the front rows. It too was contagious, and soon most of the audience in the huge, stuffy room chuckled their approval.

"I'm just going to sit down for a bit." Dowling dragged the heavy microphone toward a stool. For a moment he struggled with lowering the elevation of the microphone and then realized his mouth was still close enough to the thing to be heard. He slapped the mike on its top. There was a slight squeal in the Hippodrome.

"Silly things, aren't they?  What do you think they'll invent next?  I'm hoping somebody is working on an artificial  leg that will just run by itself.  You know, you push a button and take off down the street faster than one of those new Ford cars."  There was more laughter and some applause on the front rows.

The bearded Dowling shifted on the stool until he felt comfortable.  "All right let me tell you what happened next."

With a grin he looked straight at a man with one missing leg.  "I even amazed myself."

*It was an uncomfortable attention equally felt by those who watched. But they stared anyway.*

# CHAPTER SIX

The E. H. Erickson company in Minneapolis had one of the nicer signs in the city. Their sign was carved in intricate detail from the best hardwoods. It was only natural. The craftsmen who worked behind the building's large windows understood the finer points of carving, shaping and sanding wood. They also knew something about leather and metal.

The E. H. Erickson artificial limb company made arms and legs for anyone willing to pay the price. "Deformity Appliances," read a smaller sign. Dowling thought the "c" in the word, "Appliances," looked more like a "g," and he wondered what "Applianges" were.

"They're going to be very stiff at first." Mr. Erickson, a former carpenter-turned-businessman, was speaking to the boy from Granite Falls in a high squeaky voice that somehow didn't fit the image of his former profession. Dowling was looking over the contraptions like a kid at Christmas.

Erickson continued, "And, Michael, because you're still growing, we're going to have to adjust them occasionally; probably even have to make you a new pair within a year or two."

Dowling was grinning at the devices. The tops were made of what Erickson called "sockets." They were produced from stiff, brown leather and acted as a sleeve to fit over his amputations.

The top socket was about six inches high with an inside diameter of about five inches. It was open in the front and was outfitted with laces very similar to those found on a common boot. It was the top socket that Dowling pulled over the stump of his left leg just above the knee. He slowly tied the laces, looking toward Erickson for his approval.

The knee and what remained of his leg

below the knee, about four inches, were placed into an "inner socket" of leather that moved within the lower "outer socket." The upper and lower sockets were held together with a metal hinge.

Dowling was told the importance of oiling the hinge to keep the legs from squeaking.

The lower portion of the legs was made of hickory. The wood was in three pieces: the leg itself, the foot and the toes. The three pieces fit nicely together in a dove-tail fashion that allowed them to move a-gainst each other. They were held together with steel pins.

Erickson was proud of the artificial limbs, but Dowling's pride had already eclipsed the manufacturer's.

"Now Mike, these are the finest available, but you must know they are going to rub at your skin. You're going to have to develop callouses. They will be sore at first. I recommend that you wear them for about an hour a day at first, then add about an hour each day until you are comfortable with them. And if you need to, place some bandages on the blisters. They are sure to come."

Michael Dowling stood up. It was the first time he had experienced his full height in nearly three years, and now he was taller than he had ever been.

*I'm a giant. Too tall. I was never this tall. This is wrong.*

The new height was almost uncomfortable. It felt wrong in a good way.

*Stilts, that's what it is, I'm on stilts.*

Erickson took Dowling by the hand and Dowling tried to take his first step.

*They don't bend, they just sit there, they don't move. They don't do anything!*

"Mike, they don't move by themselves. You have to use your upper leg to sort of kick the wooden leg into place. It will come easier when you develop the proper muscles."

Dowling kicked with his upper right leg but the lower right leg promptly slid out from beneath him and he fell on his side. The fall caused the entire leg to pull away from the stump. The left leg remained in place, but at an angle that looked more like a broken, wooden soldier than a teenage boy.

"I'll get it sir, don't you worry about me. I'll be walking by the end of the week." Dowling smiled and began to reattach the errant leg. He was genuinely excited and wanted the man who had given him the chance to be whole again, to know how much he appreciated it.

"Thank you, Mr. Erickson. They really are nice. They... they're beautiful. I'll be doing things on these new legs that you'll be proud of." Dowling felt better than he had in years. There was a giddy feeling of excitement overtaking every part of him. "I'll write you and let you know how they are doing for me."

Erickson smiled. "I'd like that. Keep me informed." He pointed at the legs. "Now, take those things off and I'll pack them for you to take with you."

Dowling's reply was almost sheepish. "Uh, if it's ok with you I think I would like to wear them out of here. I think I'd like to walk right up to my front door like this." He chuckled, "I must be about seven feet tall."

If it's possible, and it is, a 17-year-old boy can be a blend of over-self-confidence and under-self-esteem. In Southern Minnesota, as in the rest of the world, teenage boys were well aware of the opposite sex. They played hard at creating a certain "aloofness" when it came to girls, but they liked the female gender and hoped, with a mighty resolve, that the feeling was somewhat mutual. It was.

Michael Dowling had thoughts of his own.

*Girls, if only they wouldn't stare. If only they might understand I'm just a regular guy. Do they talk to me just because they feel sorry for me? Or is there a small chance they might really like me.*

Dowling had taken a room close to the Carleton College campus. His dog Silver continued to live with the Larsons. He missed the dog and, whenever possible, caught rides to see the companion who had weathered the blizzard with him.

For a short time he had labored over short letters to Sarah Larson. They were always hard for him to compose and he was certain they were awkward to read. Eventually Sarah had become interested in a boy in Renville. It hurt, but only for a short time. Dowling had a painful understanding that dating and marriage were experiences that may never be his.

Charlie, his horse, had been sold to help pay for rent. He stalled the actual sale for as long as was possible. The pony that had helped him through two summers of herding cattle had been purchased by a boy about his age. The kid, he guessed his parents had given him the money, had slapped the currency into his hand and simply rode away without so much as even looking back.

But Charlie did.

Never would Dowling forget that horse looking back over its shoulder. The look in its black eyes said, *What's happening Mike, why are you doing this? Hey, come get this guy off of me. I thought it was just me and you. Come on Mike!*

When nobody was watching, Dowling cried. The loss of his horse had been another cruel amputation, and its pain was no less than that suffered when his own flesh had been cut away.

Dowling stood at the bottom of the ten stairs that led to the Carleton College building that housed his chemistry class. Walking up the hill to the campus was a feat by itself. But negotiating stairs was the biggest challenge.

*Ten of them, here we go again.*

He had accomplished the task a few times before, always with great effort.

"Hooph... hooph... hooph..." His breathing was as stilted as his legs as he slowly pulled himself along the steel handrail. He remembered the walk from his straw bed to the front porch of that farmhouse nearly three years before. The sensation of balancing on frozen, stilt-like legs rushed into his mind again.

*Mike, the man on stilts. The performer who can do anything on stilts.*

He struggled on, feeling sorry for himself. "Hooph, squeak, hooph, squeak, hooph, squeak." He had tried butter, fat and petroleum oil, and still the metal hinges and sockets squeaked.

*How am I ever going to hide the fact that I have artificial legs if they don't stop squeaking?*

Kick, hop, kick, hop. It was more a dance than a walk, and stairs required a movement that was more an athletic endeavor than a simple stroll to class.

*NO, NO! Come on... not here.*

The hinge in Dowling's right leg had frozen up. It wouldn't bend. Mike tried desperately to balance, but the unyielding hinge caused the stilt, that was his leg, to push him over. He fell to his side, then onto his back, and then, like a clumsy rolling pin, he spooled across the final four steps to the landing below. A chemistry book and four or five papers shuffled to a stop near his face.

People were watching.

Two girls were first to arrive. "Mike, Michael are you all right?"

Dowling was becoming very good on his wooden legs, but the occasional frozen hinge almost always meant a fall. Michael coped with it, but there was embarrassment.

He never did tell anyone that it was a malfunction of the device. He simply allowed people to think that it was his lack of coordination, and that always hurt more than the falls.

*Girls! Why is it always the girls that see me in these awkward positions. Girls, just go away. I'll be OK.*

His words bore no resemblance to his thoughts. "Hi ladies." He looked up into their faces. "Just studying the ants this morning." He went through the motion of sweeping a group of the imaginary insects into his hand. "I always get a better look at them when I sneak up on them like this. It's for biology. Have you done your ant studies yet?"

The girls laughed.

Michael Dowling was a tease who enjoyed making others laugh. But, when uninvited laughs came it hurt.

And then there was the hurt that came from the raw and open blisters, a result of the constant rubbing between flesh and the wooden and leather sockets.

The most painful of the hurts,

however, came from people who somehow thought Michael Dowling's ears had also been amputated.

The classrooms at Carleton College smelled mostly of chalk and cheap perfume. The girls at the school didn't have much use for the chalk, but they loved the perfume and used it whenever they could afford it. And that seemed to be almost always.

Dowling's circle of friends was always expanding. But the war to "mix," to really "get-in" and be part of the group, to become "unnoticeable" was fought in small battles on a daily basis.

On this autumn morning Dowling hobbled to a seat in the third row and plopped down with a noticeable sigh of relief. It was only the third meeting of this class, and two male students who didn't know Michael, conversed in low voices. "Hey, you won't believe it. Take a look, the guy that fell down the stairs. Not only is his arm gone, but both legs are gone; made of wood. He doesn't have any legs. Look, look at him."

"Wow, you're right," was the reply

from the second student. "The guy is some kind of a freak. A circus freak. I don't believe it."

Dowling swallowed hard, he had been through this thing before.

*Mean people. I know I'm a sight to see. Yeah, probably a freak of sorts, but don't these guys know I can hear. They couldn't be that mean!*

He adeptly pulled a pencil from his pocket and wrote on a small piece of paper. Forcing a strange smile, he handed the note to a nearby girl and motioned for her to pass the paper to the two boys.

Hesitantly the boys unfolded the paper and began reading the words neatly written across it: "The legs went to a bear, the arm was eaten by a shark. But guess what? I still have both ears, and they work just fine."

Both boys looked at Dowling at the same time. He was flipping at his right ear with his right hand, his lips pursed tightly together as he shook his head up and down in an affirmative gesture. The boys, struggling to hide their embarrassment, pushed weak smiles onto their faces. They sat back in silence.

Dowling knew he would introduce himself to them after the class.   *What else is there?  I won't hide, I can't run, I'll just meet them.  I'll make them like me.*

"Hi!  Michael Dowling is my name." He extended his deformed right hand.  One of them, with noticeable caution, took the hand and shook it.  "Uh, I'm Erick Johansen." There was an awkward silence.

The other boy, not knowing what to do, said something he hadn't planned on.  "I, er, we're going roller skating this afternoon, do you want to go?"

Dowling was surprised.  He was caught for a moment with nothing to say. Erick tried to help the situation.  "Oh, uh, you won't have to skate... but come on anyway."

"Thanks, I'd like to go."  Dowling was still shaking Erick's hand.

The skating rink was a dark place with a low ceiling and a group of unpainted wooden benches lining its perimeter.  The hardwood floors bore the traces of numerous years of hard wheels pressing into its grain. A faint smell of perspiration and leather greeted those who entered.

Lawrence O'Dea, the manager of the roller skating rink, was Mike's friend. They got along very well. Larry never played like he couldn't see the wilted stumps and missing fingers. He simply accepted them and treated Dowling as his equal. In fact, Mike believed he detected a certain awe from Lawrence O'Dea.

"Hi, Mike, you gonna strap some wheels on today?"

"Maybe I will," said Dowling with an exaggerated tone of self-confidence, although he had no intention of skating.

Erick, who hours earlier had ridiculed Dowling, was stunned by the response. "You're gonna try to roller skate?" It was an honest comment and Dowling knew it.

"Maybe." This time he wasn't sure of his intentions.

Dowling leaned against a railing and watched as classmates and others circled the aging rink. It was late in the day and his blisters were nagging him with an ongoing chant of piercing heat. He noticed a new phonograph perched on a small table, struggling to be heard. Its faint sounds were a novelty, and a number of students sat next to it, watching and listening.

*Greek History test tomorrow. Was it 546 BC or 446 BC? Croesus was overthrown by Cyrus the Great. Darius led a group of soldiers against... or was it Mardonius....*

Academics was never far from the college freshman's mind. While other students played at tennis and golf, Dowling crammed as many classes as possible into his short time at the prestigious school.

"Here, try these." O'Dea was standing next to him holding out a pair of haggard looking boots with wheels attached to the bottom.

A laugh puffed from Dowling's mouth. "Oh, I don't know... I don't know how we would even hook them up."

"We can do it," was O'Dea's instant reply.

"Come on, Larry, do you think?" But

Michael was already sitting down inspecting the inside of the skate.

Dowling knew he was once again the center of attention. It was an uncomfortable attention equally felt by those who watched. But they stared anyway. It was the thing to do. Here was the college freshman, the one with no legs and one arm, getting ready to skate.

Dowling was in the habit of forgiving those who stared; but he knew he hadn't become oblivious to the curious looks directed his way, and the whispers that were all too easy to hear. *But I do forgive them.* He knew that was a huge step toward becoming "normal."

The thoughts came quickly now. They shot through him like a spray of bullets.

*I don't want to skate. I don't need this. I've been laughed at enough. I can do just fine in life without skating. Just gracefully tell them you will try another time. Not today! Come on Mike, you don't have to be the bumbling circus freak again. Step back. Another time. Don't do it now!*

But he did.

Dowling laughed nervously as his hickory feet were placed into the boots. Rags were wedged-in to help fill the void where ankles and toes normally fit.

He pulled himself to the railing. It occurred to him that this was one of those moments that would define his life.

*Finding the straw bed, the kitchen table, lying on the oil cloth, the Yellow Medicine County Courthouse. And now the roller rink!*

He looked around at the group of people. He knew they meant well, but *this wasn't going to work, was it?*

Wham, slap. He wasn't expecting to fall quite so fast. He was holding the railing. But he fell anyway. No one laughed. That made it more uncomfortable. Several came to help him up. But he only built a wry, self-mocking smile and pulled himself to his full height.

It was as if the whole world had

stopped to watch the struggle of man over wood. There was silence. *Too much silence,* thought Dowling.

He moved carefully now, the ancient wheels rolling in a jerky fashion. Wooph! He was down again. "Hey, Larry, you've given me some bogus wheels here. They aren't working right, this some kind of a trick?" He laughed. Everyone laughed, and like a shattering icicle, the tension was broken.

Dowling lost count of the times he fell. Four or five times he stopped to reattach his legs. Usually it was the left one. The blisters howled at him. He no longer was the center of attention. He struggled on his own. The skaters had grown weary of watching the pathetic spectacle.

The rink was becoming empty. O'Dea realized that it was only 15 minutes to closing time. "Hey, Mike," he yelled across the rink. "I gotta be closing up."

Dowling hollered back, "Can I come back tomorrow?" He had managed one and a half revolutions of the rink.

"Of course, anytime."

Dowling did go back. The next day and for three weeks after that. He learned to skate. He skated better than he walked. The fluid motion of the wheels gave him a feeling of freedom he once believed had permanently abandoned him. The boy with the new legs was becoming good at something again. His confidence soared.

*I can do it! I knew it! I can be like everyone else. Come on world, I'm ready. Make way for Michael Dowling. There is nothing I can't do.*

One month after his baptism of wheels, with skates slung over his left shoulder, he approached Lawrence O'Dea.

"Larry, I'd like to work for you here after school."

"You think?"

"Hey, you know me. I've worked on riverboats, in coal yards, in wheat fields, on cattle drives. I've sold magazine subscriptions; even sold pictures of my wooden legs, if you can believe that. And I'll never do that again. That was a mistake, I was trying to gain sympathy, Larry."

He gathered his thoughts, wondering why he felt it suddenly necessary to deliver this impromptu speech to his friend.  He knew why.  He was shedding himself of the years of self-pity and anger.  He was grad-uating.  He had to tell someone.

"But now, Larry, I'd like the chance to work here. I think I can do it."

Lawrence O'Dea's response was warm and genuine. He smiled and put a hand on Dowling's shoulder.  "I think I could use you.  Yeah... maybe you could manage the place one or two nights a week."

He liked Larry O'Dea. Nice guy. He liked himself today.  He was feeling good; feeling like he was becoming the old Mike Dowling again.  He took a deep breath while smiling at the ceiling. He patted the wheels of one of the dangling skates, pursed his lips together in a tight smile  and looked the rink manager directly in the eyes.

"Larry, I'd like to manage the rink, but I think I can also TEACH... skating."

*"My mother told me it was a glimpse of God's mingling of mercy and justice."*

# CHAPTER SEVEN

Dowling sat in the office of his small home. An ambitious ray of sunshine was illuminating a lazy performance of dust particles. A picture of a mallard duck was hanging on the cream-colored wall. Dowling thought he might like to go duck hunting. He was working on the matter, but today his mind was a thick jam of thoughts and memories. He was cleaning out his desk and was in no great hurry.

Until this morning Dowling hadn't realized how many letters he had received from students and parents. It seemed the majority, in the current stack, neatly piled in front of him, were dated within the last year. He had been the principal at East Granite

Falls High School for the past three years and he smiled at the memory.

After an incredible two terms at Carleton College, Michael Dowling had been recognized as having achieved what most students gained in three, even four years. He began teaching in various frontier schools, laughing and smiling his way into the hearts of hundreds of eager students. It seemed the young were always more apt to be blind to his disabilities.

His face brightened as he came upon the picture of a young boy, a former student, holding a baseball bat.

*Bill Nelson, what's he doing now? Billy organized a group of students, pushed me down the street in that little wooden cart. Helped get me to school a couple of times when the blisters were too painful to wear the legs. Whatever happened to Bill?*

A letter from Prudence Tasker fell from a folder. Prudence was a frail, self-conscious girl in a sixth grade class. It was a recent letter written to thank Dowling for a kindness from two years earlier.

*How will I ever forget that morning? I kind of found myself in a trap, didn't I?*

Dear Mr. Dowling,

*You probably have forgotten something that I will never forget; and since you are about to leave town, I wanted to write and thank you.*

*It was a hot spring day. The first flies of the season were buzzing through the classroom and most of the kids were having a hard time concentrating on studies. Many of the students were dropping pencils and making a commotion as they picked up their pencils over and over.*

The 19-year-old school teacher was clearly annoyed. Dowling rose from behind his desk and walked with ease to the front of the classroom. His voice thundered. "The next one who drops a pencil must come up here and place it on this chair." He tapped at a chair with a long measuring stick.

*Mr. Dowling, I was scared to death that I would probably drop my pencil. I held it so tightly that the blood left my fingers.*

159

"What if I dropped my pencil?" The thought was very scary to me. And then it happened. My slate pencil slipped out of my fingers and fell to the floor. It broke into several pieces. It was badly broken, but not as badly as my heart. Everybody turned to watch me. I felt a terrible shame. I wished I was dead.

"Well," said Michael Dowling in a voice that was kind and soft, "I'm afraid Prudence, you will have to come up here and put your pencil on the chair."

I remember gathering up the pieces of the pencil. I grabbed onto the desk and tried to stand. I was burning with embarrassment and an awful shame. I wondered why this had happened to me. And you just looked at me as if you were going to cry.

I could make out your face, but that aisle of desks to the front of the class looked to be about a mile long. Tears ran down my face. Clinging to the desks, I tried to walk down that aisle. I could hear some of the kids laughing.

And then a wondrous thing happened. I saw that teacher, you Mr. Dowling, coming to meet me, carrying the chair in your hands. You sat it down gently beside me and said, "There, lay your pencil there. I know you didn't mean to drop it. Now it's all right with both of us."

Mr. Dowling, nobody, even with real hands and feet could have been kinder. My mother told me later that it was a glimpse of God's mingling of mercy and justice.

Thank you for teaching me to like geography and history and for making school fun. Good luck as the new superintendent of schools over in Renville County.

Memories and reminiscing, they have a way of forcing one to take stock of their life.

Dowling, although only 22, had a mental maturity far greater than many of his older supervisors in the educational community. He believed he was beginning to know something about success and its definition.

He smiled as he remembered departing from a lesson on mathematics to pontificate, *yes that's the word, pontificate,* on the definition of success.

He believed the word's definition was happiness. But happiness, he guessed, was an elusive thing that was defined in many ways. Dowling knew there were those who chased success, who believed happiness would one day be theirs. He also believed that those who believed they would <u>one day</u> have happiness probably never would.

He understood well that being happy was an everyday thing. It was a frame of mind, a feeling. He thought he was happy. He believed he was successful. Maybe not successful like wealthy businessmen or famous politicians; but for the time being, he had achieved the things he would liked to have had even with legs.

He didn't have a wife, that was true, but he had faced the challenges of providing for himself and had done rather well.

And now he was prepared to begin the assignment of superintendent of Renville County Schools. The board of education, impressed with his array of skills, had hired Dowling one week earlier.

He was on his third set of artificial legs now. They far excelled the first pair of ill-fitting legs on which he had learned to roller skate. They were even better than the pair he had rode horses with a year earlier. The new pair of hardwoods allowed him a walk that was almost undiscernible from others. It was a scarce thing to hear them squeak. And the blisters of bygone years were nothing more than reminders of how good things had become.

Michael had been fitted with his first artificial arm two years earlier and he was beginning to enjoy a new game: deception.

He enjoyed "deceiving" people into thinking he had no limitations. An arm with a special hand-type apparatus, instead of a hook, was occasionally employed to further the illusion. On several occasions he had placed white gloves on both hands. In this array, Michael Dowling was magically transformed into a man who had never spent a night in a fierce blizzard with minus fifty degree temperatures.

He liked the illusion. But he only played with it. He had no shame of his artificial limbs and, on most occasions, he used the arm with the functional steel hook that allowed him a dexterity that felt very much like the left hand he remembered from what now was becoming an entire lifetime ago.

Dowling walked briskly up the stairs of the Renville County High School. The stilted feeling of earlier years was still there, but it was very natural, and he moved with a dignity that belied the steel, leather and wood beneath the pant legs of his cotton suit.

Once seated at a neatly arranged desk in his oak office he reached for a folder of papers. His concentration on the problem of finding a teacher for the Sioux Indian students near Franklin was interrupted.

"Mr. Dowling, there is a Mrs. Mumford here to see you." His assistant, an older woman, had entered the room.

"Alice Mumford?"

"Yes, that's right"

"Didn't she buy a house in Bird Island this past spring?"

"Yes," was his assistant's reply. Dowling was sure he had heard about the lady. She had quickly earned the title of town gossip and busybody. He guessed he was about to find out if the labels were justified.

"Do you know what she wants?"

"She says she has some kind of a problem. Says she needs you to talk to the parents of an 11-year-old boy."

This was one of the things Dowling detested about working in administration. This thing with Alice Mumford sounded like the sort of thing that would probably steal time from something more important, and a small bale of cotton began to grow in his stomach.

"What kind of problem, do you know?" Dowling was scanning a list of applicants for a teaching position.

"She claims he has a wooden foot. He lost his real one in a farming accident."

The young superintendent pushed the list of applicants away. His eyes riveted on the older woman.

"What does she want me to tell them?"

The woman was a bit nervous now. She wasn't sure of what Dowling's response might be. "Well, she uh, thinks the boy shouldn't play baseball on the school team. She thinks it might hurt the boy. She thinks it might hurt the team."

But Dowling wasn't angry. He appeared to be slightly amused. An almost devilish grin appeared on his handsome, sun-tanned face.

*She apparently doesn't know me very well.*

"Give me a few moments and then send her in."

As soon as the messenger had left the room, Dowling leaped from his chair. The grin had grown in size and the cotton bale was dissolving fast. He quickly took off his suit jacket, removed his left arm and replaced it with the device that included the wooden hand. He replaced his suit coat, pulled on a pair of white gloves and began reading through papers on his desk.

"Mr. Dowling, I'm Alice Mumford." Her arrival was timed almost perfectly. Dowling rose to his feet and greeted the middle-aged woman. "Please have a seat."

Mrs. Mumford wore too much make-up. Her perfume reminded him of the classrooms at Carleton College. Her dark hair was secured in a tight knot at the rear of her head and her voice was high and scratchy.

*The labels are correct.*

But then he quickly chastised himself for the thought.

"Mr. Dowling..."

"Please, just call me Michael. Mr. Dowling somehow sounds too old for me." The young administrator was trying to make his visitor feel at ease.

"OK, Michael, we have a little problem over in Bird Island at the grade school. I think you'll understand that something needs to be done about it."

"What is it, Alice? Tell me about it."

"Well it's Bobby Randall, he's 11-years-old and he has a wooden foot. He lost his real foot in a farming accident. A horse pulled a metal plow right over it. A dreadful thing. Who'd have thought a plow could do that kind of damage, but it did. The thing was so awfully sharp. It cut right through his foot. I wasn't living there when it happened, but I've heard all about it a thousand times."

"How's the boy doing?" Dowling was genuinely interested. He hadn't heard of the accident.

"Oh, he appears to be OK. You know, he can walk to school all right. But you and I both know he's never going to be like the

other boys. There is just no way. And now...
now he wants to play baseball. And I really
think he could hurt himself even more. He
could very easily hurt the other boys, might
put the other members of the team in some
kind of jeopardy, don't you think?"

Dowling could taste the heat boiling
into his cheeks. He promised himself he was
going to be able to handle this situation. In
fact, maybe he could even enjoy it.

The town gossip continued. "The poor
boy, the poor little creature, he has his mind
set on playing baseball. We really need to do
something, don't you think?"

He didn't break. He had an idea.

"Alice, will you follow me? I want to
show you something."


It was a warm day. Already the temperature was in the eighties. There was a
chance this might become one of those rare
Minnesota days when the red line on the
thermometer went north of the ninety degree
mark.

Kitty-corner to the school building
was a large, vacant lot. It had never been
built upon because much of the lot was a steep

hill. Not a huge hill. Its elevation was maybe eighty-five feet above the surrounding ground. But in Renville County it was big. In winter hundreds of laughing, squealing children with a variety of sleds were attracted to the snow-covered mound.

"Up there," Dowling pointed to the top of the hill. "I want to show you something up there." Alice Mumford wondered what the view would allow them that couldn't be seen from their present location. She was finding it hard to read the young, new county superintendent.

*He was a strange man,* she thought. *He's got gloves on, and a jacket and it's hot out here!*

A narrow trail switched its way to the hill's summit. Within moments, the lady with the heavy coating of rouge was breathing with some difficulty.

Dowling walked, in the lead, with a steady movement. "How you doin', Mrs. Mumford?" Alice thought she heard a bit of a tease in Dowling's voice. "Oh, I'm just fine, beautiful day."

She had done it. She was able to get

the six words out without sounding winded. It wasn't easy. She had to sort of hold her breath while talking. She paid for it when the sentence was over. A half-dozen short gasps came from her mouth as she stopped for a moment.

"Anything wrong?" Dowling asked.

"No," there was heavy breathing. "No, uh, just an old dancing injury. It's my ankles... but I'm OK."

The march upward continued, neither saying anything. When they arrived at the top, Michael stopped, looked at the distant horizon, spun around on an artificial heel and looked closely at the red-faced lady. He smiled. He felt a little sorry for her. It had been a tough climb for Alice Mumford.

"I want you to see something."

Chest heaving, Alice was searching the horizon. "What is it? Where?"

"Right here," came Dowling's reply.

With his right gloved hand he began pulling up his right pant leg in a crawl-like movement that looked something like a curtain going up on a Broadway play. Slowly the wooden leg with its leather and metal attachments was revealed. It looked stark and functional in the morning sun like a tool or farm implement. Dowling hitched his cuff onto a metal rivet that held leather to wood. He glanced quickly at the lady's face.

The red rouge was losing its battle to cover a growing pale of ghostly white. Her eyes were as big as quarters and her bottom lip was beginning to quiver.

In a movement that was not unlike a magician cleverly performing the final part of a great magic act, he gracefully revealed the second leg.

The look on Alice Mumford's face was his payoff. He knew he was enjoying it too much and thought that the county superintendent of schools should maintain some dignity and professionalism.

*Dowling, you promised never to use your legs and arm for sympathy.* He answered himself immediately. *But this isn't sympathy, this is a lesson. But maybe I'm enjoying it too much.*

He spoke with a smile and self-confidence that flowed together. "Had them for over five years now. Lost my legs when I was only 14-years-old. They were froze off in a blizzard."

*Should I pull off the gloves? No, she looks like she's about to pass out.*

"This hill is a lot steeper than any old baseball field, Mrs. Mumford." His eyes were smiling now. His entire face was lit as bright as the morning sun. Dowling took Alice Mumford's hand in his. "That Bobby Randall sounds like a fighter. I'd get him on that team as fast as I could."

He felt sorry for the sweating lady who was wrestling to find the right thing to say. Her reply was an exasperated stutter.

"Oh, oh, I'm so... so suh sorry."

"Don't be sorry, Mrs. Mumford. Go back and get that boy on the playing field. There's a good chance he'll help win that Bird Island school a county championship!"

...*his whole insides filled with a thousand flapping moths. His mouth was dry. He swallowed hard. There was almost a taste of salt. "No, I can't do it now... yes I can!"*

# CHAPTER EIGHT

Maybe it was the peculiar odor that attracted people to the offices of the Renville *STAR-FARMER*. There were always three or four people standing around talking about the weather, the price of wheat and, of course, the day's news. The offices of the weekly newspaper smelled of industry, ink and paper.

Today it also smelled of scandal.

In the back room a pressman, William Reid, stood alongside a noisy, rattling device that was laboring to produce a sheet of paper covered with a variety of large and small black words.

"Here it is," he finally yelled out. "Here's the first one."

Dowling, now in his late twenties had

purchased the newspaper a few years before, had sold it and now had bought it back, this time with William A. Reid as his partner.

"Let's have a look at it, Bill." Michael and his partner walked towards each other on the uneven wooden floor. "This one is going to make or break us."

A headline, at least two inches high, screamed out the news: "FINANCIAL FRAUD AT MINNEAPOLIS FIRM."

Dowling responded to the paper by touching the stub of his thumb onto the fresh ink, checking for smudges and then setting the paper on a table.

"It's too bad a company like Parsons & Willig figures it's beyond the law. This story will probably kill them but the public deserves to know. People have invested money there, hard-working people who deserve some kind of security."

Reid had observed an attractive young woman looking through the front window of the offices.

Dowling continued, "It's just part of the business, Bill. Journalists have a responsibility to the public to report this kind of stuff. The big papers in Minneapolis are going..."

Reid wasn't hearing anything his

partner was saying. The girl at the window had most of his attention. She was making faces trying to get him to laugh. It was working.

"Sorry, Mike... take a look outside."

Dowling turned to see an employee of *THE GRANITE FALLS TRIBUNE* from the next county.

It was Jennie Bordewich.

The petite young woman, now 22-years-old, had known Michael Dowling since the time he was a 15-year-old boy being pushed about town in a baby buggy. She had developed into an attractive woman and was being pursued by a number of men.

Miss Bordewich was invited into Dowling's office. The walls in the cramped room were a storm of numerous papers impaled on nails. Dowling slipped into a barrel-like chair as Jennie was motioned to a smaller seat.

The woman spoke first.

"Are you still planning to leave for Atlanta on the 25th of September?"

She knew the answer to the question, but she asked it anyway. She and Dowling had communicated for more than a dozen years, mostly in a casual, two-or-three-times-a-year way. But recently, because of their careers and their mutual membership in the Minnesota Editorial Association, they were seeing each other much more frequently.

Dowling replied as he put his hand on hers. "Nothing in the world would keep me from going to Atlanta, unless, of course, you decided to back out."

The National Editorial Association was planning its annual convention in the South's largest city and many journalists would attend.

*Something happening here Dowling. There are feelings here that are awfully strong. You've got a paper to run, back off a little. You have things to do. No time for women. But this was different, Jennie was different.*

But then those feelings had been there for a long time, hadn't they? There had been too many picnics, too many canoe trips at the lake and too many dinners to deny that something was happening here, and the former school teacher/superintendent turned real estate investor/newspaperman knew he was being consumed by something he couldn't control. Strange, he thought, how he really didn't care to control it.

*Funny, isn't it; I feel I am in complete control of my destiny. I will work to achieve anything I want. But, this... this thing with Jennie is out of control. It's a runaway train.*

*But is it really Michael Dowling? You know what you want; you're totally in control here. Henry Bordewich may not like me... and I'm sure it's my artificial legs... but maybe he will in time.*

"Stone Mountain" it was called. Like a gigantic slumbering elephant it rose out of the woods; about an hour trip from the commotion of Atlanta. During late summer the place seemed to issue a new type of flower every week. About the time one wilted away, a replacement, even better than the last would mix with the green grass to provide a living quilt that attracted bees, small animals and numerous people, including Michael Dowling and Jennie Bordewich.

The two rode bicycles down a dirt lane. The wheels wobbled in a hypnotic fashion as they pedaled. The hard tires occasionally smashed tiny dirt clods causing minuscule, powdery explosions. Dowling's bike had a large wicker basket attached to a rattling steel fender. The basket contained bread, fruit and two small bags. One was filled with licorice and the other contained gumdrops.

The warm, late-summer air mixed with the fragrance of flowers created an exotic mood that was not lost on the two bikers. "Makes you feel like screaming out, doesn't it Jennie?"

"It does, Michael, it's a beautiful day. The sky is a different blue from back home."

Dowling enjoyed physical exercise. He loved to ride horses and claimed there wasn't a creature with four legs he couldn't handle. And bicycles; they were more difficult to ride than a horse but the challenge was invigorating.

Jennie pulled up alongside Michael for a brief moment. She smiled in a way that always made Dowling feel good. Then with a slight, girlish laugh she overtook the 29- year-old man and pedaled into the lead position.

Dowling watched her from behind, taking particular notice of her dark hair.

*Jennie Bordewich, what are you doing to me?*

A small cloud drifted over Dowling's thoughts as he remembered the day Jennie's father, Henry Bordewich, stopped him on the street. The conversation started with the normal things: talk about the newspaper business and the weather. Dowling was surprised when the conversation changed.

"Now Mike, I know Jennie and you have taken a sort of fancy for each other."

"Well, yes, I do like her, and I sort of hope she likes me."

"Well, I think she does." He paused and looked at a passing carriage. He swallowed and continued without looking back at the young newspaper owner. "I kind of think she might be a little too young for you, Mike. I've got nothing against you, you know that. I was happy to help you back then with the county commissioners and all, but I just think she might be a bit young, that's all."

*But that wasn't all, was it. Henry was wondering about me being a cripple. He thinks I'm a cripple. I haven't yet proved to him that I am like everyone else. Jennie's father can be won over... I think he can. I'll prove it to him, and everyone else... I AM NOT A CRIPPLE!*

Henry Bordewich made Dowling a little uneasy. He knew he was good at making friends and when he failed, as in Henry's case, it bothered him.

A sudden burst of resolve to find Jennie's father's respect was transferred to Dowling's wooden legs. He pedaled hard and quickly passed Jennie.

"Am I going too fast?" Michael was yelling over his shoulder at the slender woman who lagged five lengths behind.

"No, not at all." Jennie Bordewich was breathing hard and intensely enjoying the experience.

"Should we go a little faster?" Dowling's enjoyment equaled Jennie's.

Jennie, pedaling with a strong rhythm, yelled to her partner. "No Michael that might not be wise with your... your," she quickly glanced at his legs then back at his face. She knew she had made a mistake and finished the sentence in nearly a whisper. "...with your legs."

Dowling immediately stopped his bike by dragging his shoes through a small dust storm. Jennie stopped alongside him.

"Wait just a minute, Johanna Bordewich."

*Ah-oh,* thought Jennie, *here comes something, a lecture or something. Get ready!*

She had sincere, deep feelings for

Dowling. She was only slightly uneasy about the artificial limbs and was coming to the realization that most of the time she didn't even see them. The young assistant editor at the *GRANITE FALLS TRIBUNE* was more aware of his professionalism, his non-stop energy and most of all, his kindness.

"Just a minute here," Dowling was only slightly out of breath, "you need to know that I'm just like any other man, except maybe a little bit better." He laughed at that.

It made Jennie feel easier. She knew he was right about being just a little bit better than any other man.

"You know I have to be a little bit better. This can be a mean world. If I'm going to survive I have to be better than the next guy. That means bicycles, too!"

Jennie spoke softly, "Michael I'm sorry, we can ride as fast as you want. I... I guess it was just a normal reaction. I'm sorry."

Dowling was affected by her apology. He leaned back on the seat of his bicycle and looked down at a small bug navigating the edge of the road. "I know you're sorry, I guess I overreacted." He looked into Jennie's sparkling dark eyes. "I don't normally do that. I guess I wanted to make sure that you,

you more than anyone else, knew what was going on in my head."

He felt an important speech coming on and realized he hadn't prepared for it. He wondered if this was the right time, the right place. The words tumbled from his dusty throat.

"You see, Jennie, I have to make sure people can see past my legs and arm."

A new thought came to him.

"You know something else... the world is full of problems, everyone's got some kind of problem. You run newspapers, like we do, and you learn about the problems of the world. My problems aren't anything compared to the homeless kids in Chicago and what about those people who have nothing to eat- grown people who can't feed their children! I've got no problems compared to them."

"I haven't told many people this, but I'd like to try to do something about some of the problems of the world. I know it may sound silly, and what can one guy do? But I am thinking of running for public office, maybe get into politics. I might run for the Legislature in St. Paul. Learning law back there in Judge Powers' office, well, maybe I can use that one day."

Dowling had immersed himself in the law books of a county Judge when he was going to high school.

Jennie's response was quick and genuine. "You would be a great congressman, Michael, I know you would."

He smiled a crooked, "thank you," and pushed his bike to the side of the road, placing it in the blanket of grass and flowers.

"All right, Jennie, I have an idea. We're going to have a bike race. From here to that big oak tree up around the bend, and then back again." He etched a line in the dirt road with the heel of his shoe. "This is the finish line."

"You're not going to beat me Michael Dowling." Jennie spoke with the energy and conviction that had attracted Dowling many years before. She continued with a hint of laughter. "You won't beat me."

"If I can't beat you, if you win," said Dowling, "you won't ever have to go out with me again."

He lowered his voice and with a tone of mock authority, he continued. "With that kind of reward, I trust you will try as hard as possible."

"What if I lose the race?" Jennie was smiling and guessing what he would say.

"If you lose and I win... well..." Dowling looked away, his whole insides filled with a thousand flapping moths. His mouth was dry. He swallowed hard. There was almost a taste of soap.

*No, I can't do it now... yes I can!*

The boy with the artificial legs, the man with the huge heart and granite spirit turned and looked at the girl he had met more than ten years earlier.

"If I win Jennie... If I win Jen... then, then you will just have to marry me. I guess we'll just have to get married, Jennie."

"Michael!" It was a squeal accompanied by tears. "I love you, I will marry you!"

In spite of his physical challenges, Jennie Bordewich knew the man who had wrapped one arm of flesh and one arm of wood around her shoulders was probably the most remarkable person she would ever know in her entire life.

Dowling won the race and was only slightly perturbed to see that Jennie's effort, even though she put up a decent facade, was only half of her capacity.

The speaker in the Hippodrome was still seated. The air had cooled as afternoon dissolved into evening in the big city. He leaned back into his chair and reached for a glass of water placed on a small table near the podium. He drank two swallows then leaned forward towards the huge audience.

"I'd like you to meet Jennie. We've been married for almost 25 years. We decided to get married right there and then, while we were at that conference in Atlanta. Jennie will you please stand up."

In the second row, a slender, brunette woman with tiny traces of gray in her hair stood. She looked around at the mammoth audience behind her. There was applause.

"Girls, why don't you stand also."

Three young women in their teens and early twenties rose to their feet, next to their mother.

"These are my three daughters." There was a slight hitch in his voice betraying some emotion. "Our first child, my son, Michael John, died in infancy. But you can see I've been blessed with three fine daughters. They are Marjorie, Kathleen and Dorothy."

"I'm happy to say, when a man has his legs froze off, he doesn't pass on to the next generation the same condition. As you can see the girls all take after their mother. They are good looking."

A moderate wave of laughter rolled through the crowded building. The front rows of disabled soldiers, then the entire audience, clapped their hands vigorously in agreement.

It was unanimous. They liked Mike Dowling and they wanted him to know it.

"Well, I did a lot of things ladies and gentlemen. Some good, some not so good. In the interest of time, I've decided to only tell you about the good things."

There was more laughter.

*"Thank you, good sir, thank you for stopping me. You have just saved my life."*

# CHAPTER NINE

Another clanging bell outside the Hippodrome seemed to punctuate the silence as Dowling wiped his forehead with his handkerchief. A man with an arm in a sling, not far from the podium, appeared to want to light a cigarette. He fumbled with the package, then, apparently in frustration, threw it into his lap.

Dowling knew he had the audience. It was a good feeling. It was a feeling of victory and power. *They're mine,* he thought. *But don't lose them. You've got a serious responsibility here, Dowling. Do it right!*

The speaker began in a coarse, uneven voice. "Most peop..." He cleared his voice.

He had been talking for well over an hour. "Most people are proud of what they have accomplished in life. I guess I'm just like everyone else in that regard. Just briefly I am going to let you know about some of the good things that have happened to me. I've been very fortunate."

"I stayed at that superintendent's job in Renville County for three years. Then, as I told you, I got into the newspaper business. After that I tried my hand at banking."

He held up his hooked left hand. "It seemed to work out OK." There was a smattering of laughter.

"I became the president of the Olivia State Bank. But don't let that fool you, it was a small bank. Still is. My fellow bankers elected me to be president of the Minnesota Bankers Association."

"It was in the election of 1900, five years after Jen and I were married, that I was elected to the Minnesota House of Representatives. I took office, and then I was very surprised to be elected to 'Speaker of the House.' That was a high honor for me that I will never forget."

"Oh don't think I didn't occasionally

try to buy favor by capitalizing on my injuries. But, I learned early... I knew that if I treated myself as if I were different from other people, the world would follow my example. I've always expected from myself no less than the next guy might expect from himself."

"Some of you know that I served for two years as secretary of the National Republican League."

"Then there was the great adventure of helping to establish the Yellowstone Trail. That road now goes from the East Coast to Livingstone, Montana; right at the entrance to the park. When I first drove it with my family in one of our first cars, about six years ago, I found it to be fascinating. We live in a beautiful country. America is better than anywhere I've been."

"Many of you know I am currently talked about as a candidate for Governor of Minnesota. If that honor comes, I will cherish it, just as I have the other opportunities that have come my way."

Dowling seemed to be ending his talk. He paused to make sure there wasn't anything he had forgotten.

"You all know that education is very important to me, and so I was very excited about my appointment to the United States Education Commission." His face brightened. He had remembered something. "And it was while serving as a Commissioner of Education for the United States Government that I had a little fun."

"Chhhhhhhhhhrrr, chhhhhhhhhhrrrr, chhhhhhhhhrrr," From the moment Mike Dowling had stepped off the boat he noticed the steady drone. It was even more noticeable than the smothering humidity. He was unsure of the origin of the noise, but it was foreign and it intrigued him. But then the entire journey had been that way. Sixteen days on a steamer out of the Port of San Francisco, and now here he was in the Philippines; the Island Republic of Sulu.

Last week during his visit to Manila he had heard the same noise.

"Chhhhhhhhhrrrr," the noise continued. It seemed to come from the sky. But he could see no birds. Dowling had hunted some wild animals in recent years. However, in spite of a hard search into the myriad of experiences stored in his mind, he still could not connect the sound with beast of fur or feather.

He believed it sounded more like some strange electric device. He resolved, before returning to the United States, he would find some answers about the buzzing, mechanical sound that was everywhere.

Commissioner Dowling had been told a combination of English and Spanish was spoken in this part of the islands, and he had seized the opportunity to be tutored in Spanish by an aging professor on board the ship.

*Even if I don't need it, it will be nice to know a little Spanish.*

His attitude toward education was typical, and he spent two hours each day pursuing the foreign language.

"Sir!" called Dowling. A man with a strange-looking bicycle approached. The rear of his bike was a small trailer that included a seat and a low-slung roof. The bike was designed for passengers and it was similar to thousands of others in the Philippine Islands

"Can you please take me to the Sultan's Palace?"

The small man, old and frail, almost leaped to attention.

*English, it works!*

To the driver of this strange taxi, this was not the normal request. "Yes sir, right away sir. To the Sultan's Palace. Please get in."

The driver guessed Dowling was an official of some kind, certainly a man of wealth. It was more than his destination that gave him away. It was his wardrobe: a white suit, white shoes and today he wore the white gloves.

Mr. Dowling had been excited to learn that gloves were worn at formal occasions in the islands. This was a formal occasion; a visit with the Sultan of Sulu to outline steps the United States was willing to take to improve the education system here.

The journey through the narrow streets was more a perilous adventure than a cab ride. Milling throngs of people, cattle, chickens and pigs formed a harrowing obstacle course that tested the skill of the aging man pedaling the strange vehicle. Dowling swayed from side to side, leaning into the turns and anticipating the moves like a jockey on a crazed mount.

"Sir, here 'tis, the Sultan's residence." They were parked in front of a flamingo-pink, stucco building. Canvas awnings shaded the open windows from a burning sun.

Dowling paid the man with what he believed was the correct number of strange-looking coins, grabbed his leather bag and stepped into the shade of the building's portico. He knocked on the heavy, mahogany door, unsure of what was to follow.

"Yes, good sir?" A man dressed in white, much like Dowling, opened the door. He was small with a gray goatee and tiny round spectacles.

"Michael Dowling, sir, United States Commissioner of Education."

"Oh yes, of course. We have been

expecting you Mr. Dowling. Won't you please come in. I am the butler, and I will show you to the Sultan's quarters."

"Chhhhhhhhrrrr," The sound inside the building was louder than he had heard before. It seemed to be coming from the left.

*What is it? What is that noise?*

Dowling was led to the right, down a long marble hallway. "Sir, please," Dowling tapped the man on his shoulder.

"Yes, what is it?"

"The noise," explained Dowling, "Can you help me? I've heard that noise since I have arrived in the islands. It's driving me crazy because I can't figure out what it is."

The small man smiled. His eyes sparkled. "Oh, I see. In the United States you do not have the... no, I will show you. Follow me."

The two men reversed direction and entered a room that contained a few items of rattan furniture, a young boy and a tight-meshed, wire box. The boy was hovering near the box tending its contents.

The small cage held a boiling mass of large green beetles. Several were clinging upside down to the top of the cage. They, it appeared, were the noisemakers. The five hundred or so others were only weaving themselves in and out of the surging mess in a never-ending frenzy.

*A young boy tending his cattle... that's all it is. They're his cattle... just a little different than my cattle 35 years ago.*

The giant bugs, about an inch-and-a-half in length, also produced an audible "grinding" sound at this close range. Dowling guessed it was produced by the sheer numbers grinding their bodies in a constant rotation.

Their shells or wings, he couldn't tell if they could fly, were covered in what looked like a pearly, emerald substance that almost appeared to be of some value, like an exotic jewelry.

The noise in the cage was continuous.

Dowling's guide raised his voice to be heard. "Beetles for the Sultan's birds." He was pleased to show him the bugs. "Rhamik, the boy, catches the beetles and keeps a fresh supply at all times for the Sultan's many parrots."

"The noise," Dowling was fascinated, "it must be made like a cricket then. By vibrating its body. Is that correct?"

"It is," replied the man. "The beetles are considered a pest by most of us. They are found throughout the islands."

Dowling smiled. The mystery had been solved. "Thank you. Thank you for your kindness."

*Just a bunch of blamed old bugs. I should have known it. Didn't I hear something like that down near Atlanta? I should have known...*

No one had ever accused Michael Dowling of having great patience. He loved to keep moving, finding the next adventure, exploring the unknown and pushing himself to new heights. Sitting in the hallway outside of the Sultan's office didn't qualify as any of those things. He had been waiting now for nearly a half hour.

Never one to waste time, Dowling had taken a small bottle of ink, a pen and two sheets of paper from his bag. He began writing in his characteristic, elegant penmanship.

*April 1900*

*My Dear Jennie*
*and Papa's Darling Baby Girl Dorothy-*

*I have been in the islands for almost a month and many are the strange things I have seen that I wish you might have seen with me.*

*Jennie, I am pleased to report that a letter from the White House has encouraged me to think that I am being considered for a high diplomatic post such as a foreign diplomat. But maybe such an honor should go to someone else. How do you think your father would feel about such an appointment? I believe I might be able to influence President McKinley into appointing your father as a foreign diplomat. I think he would do very well in such a post. Maybe even in Norway. He might even start to like me...*

"Mr. Dowling, I'm so sorry for the delay."

It was the butler. He looked at his watch. Forty-five minutes since he had sat down.

The tiny man had been passing back and forth like a nervous pigeon looking into the Sultan's office mentioning the presence of Dowling, then leaving, then reappearing. It had almost been laughable, but now Dowling's limited patience was wearing down. He blew on the fresh ink, waved the paper in the air and placed it, with the ink and pen back into his bag. He would finish the letter later.

The little man was once more in the Sultan's office, and Dowling could hear the conversation very well.

"But your excellency, he has come a long way. He is with the United States Government, a Commissioner of Education and he has come to help our people. He has been waiting for a very long time."

Dowling believed it was the Sultan's voice he heard next. "Yes, but I am very busy. Why don't you just feed him a nice meal and send him away. Please, just get rid of him."

Dowling felt the dull throb of rejection that always lit the fires of motivation within him. He rose to his feet and entered the room without an invitation.

The Sultan was a man of moderate stature. He was nearly naked, wearing only a white cloth, wrapped like a diaper, around his midsection. On his bare shoulder was a large colorful scarf. Perched on the scarf was a huge green and yellow parrot.

The bird's head turned quickly as Dowling entered. It squawked its disapproval at the intruder, then turned back as the Sultan placed another large beetle into the bird's orange beak.

Dowling didn't wait for an introduction, with a warm smile he extended his right, gloved hand.

"Sir, it's an honor to meet you. My name is Michael Dowling. William McKinley, President of the United States of America, has sent me to meet with you about your education system."

The Sultan shook his visitor's hand. The butler motioned for Dowling to sit down and then left the room. The Sultan said nothing but continued to feed the giant bird.

"A beautiful bird Your Excellency. What kind of parrot is that?" Dowling tried to get the Sultan's attention.

"Just a parrot. Now you know I am a busy man. Can you please come back another time?" The arrogant man refused to look directly at the Commissioner.

*OK, Mr. Sultan, time for some magic.* Dowling's thoughts caused him to smile. *Why not? This might be fun!*

The Sultan didn't see Dowling reach into his left sleeve to begin removing his left arm. But when the man from the United States slowly pulled the entire arm from the sleeve, he was watching. There was no doubt, he did get a good look at the wooden arm with it's make-believe hand as it was placed on his desk.

The Sultan watched Dowling very closely now, with wide eyes. Just as slowly the Sultan's guest rolled up his left pant leg.

*Yes the circus man, the circus freak here to entertain one and all, young and old, large and small.*

With great skill the performance continued. Dowling had this man's full attention and he loved it. He began humming a favorite showtune. He thought it added a dramatic flare. When he threw his left leg over his right shoulder, the Sultan leaped to his feet, his mouth wide open .

*He's losing it,* thought Dowling, *he's slipping away, may go into a coma.*

The Sultan said nothing.

Dowling carefully removed his right leg and held it out for the Sultan to take.

"No, no, Mr. Dowling. This is not necessary. Let us talk." The Sultan was eager to stop the human disintegration that was taking place in front of him.

*I should probably stop now. I've got his attention.*

But he didn't.

Dowling smiled and placed his right hand on top of his head. With an insane smile he began the motion of unscrewing his head from his body.

The Sultan leaped toward his visitor. In a colorful explosion of feathers, beetles and squawks, the giant bird tumbled from the Sultan's shoulder.

With his face linen white, the Sultan grabbed Dowling's arm and pulled it from his head. "No, no, please do not do that. You must not do that. I see you are magic, I am most happy and honored to talk with you."

Dowling feigned great relief and sighed with mock exasperation. "Thank you, good sir, thank you for stopping me." For this brief performance thousands of miles from home, he had become a professional actor. "I think you have just saved my life."

Sulu's Sultan backed away in a state of shock. "Please allow me to put on some proper attire. I will be glad... most happy to hear you."

Dowling asked if the Sultan could return his arm to him and then, in a smooth authoritarian voice, announced his agenda.

"Thank you, good sir, and upon your return, another type of magic. It is called ED-U-CA-TION."

*"I came here tonight expecting to see a bunch of cripples."*

# CHAPTER TEN

The man seated center stage in the Hippodrome was beginning to look weary. He had been talking for almost two hours. Normally he would have finished long ago, but tonight he had felt a need to continue. Dowling, always sensitive to his audience, had observed only two people leaving the room. He correctly perceived that his words were of some importance.

In other talks similar to this one his main objective was to inspire men and women who faced challenges that had deflated and darkened their lives. He had spoken in England, Scotland, Wales, Belgium and France.

Tonight was different.

Somehow he felt an additional importance to this particular evening in the great darkened room in New York City. Never had he spoken before a group this size. Never had a Supreme Court Justice introduced him, and never had he looked into the eyes of so many soldiers with so many injuries. Somehow he felt that perhaps there may not be many more opportunities such as this.

He knew he had prepared his whole life for this speech, this night in the Hippodrome, and he knew the most important part was here.

The boy who had spent the night in a blizzard with only the dog that now, forty years later, was nothing but a bright memory, rose slowly to his feet. He wanted to get closer to the men with the injuries. He walked to the edge of the large stage, carrying the microphone with him. He looked into the eyes of a boy who looked no older than nineteen. He was missing his right arm. His strong legs were crossed in front of him.

"Now let me be honest with you," Dowling's voice, amplified in the PA system, was clear and resonant. "I came here tonight expecting to see a bunch of cripples. But so far as I can see, I'm about the only first class cripple in the room. How many of you have lost both feet?"

Two of the disabled soldiers near the center of the row spoke uneasily to each other. The others remained silent.

"How many of you have lost both hands? Well, boys, you aren't in my class at all. I've lost both legs, one arm and most of the other hand."

Dowling paused and walked five paces to the left. "They put me to sleep with chloroform." He felt a dry lump grow rapidly in the back of his throat. His voice quivered slightly.

*No... no... you can do it, you can get through this.*

The size of the audience and its riveting attention was, somehow, bringing back emotions that had not surfaced during other speeches.

"They put me to sleep with chloroform and when I woke up I felt sorry for myself. Oh yeah, people stared. They pitied. Some laughed. Most just turned away; they didn't want to have to look at me."

Dowling looked up at the ceiling and then back at his audience. He wiped at his left eye and continued with a stronger voice.

"Now you boys lost a leg or an arm fighting in a great cause, a World War. You were bringing peace and freedom to the world, making sure we could continue as a strong country, these United States of America. And I... I lost my legs and arm and fingers just fighting a blamed old blizzard."

He looked at his one metal hand and his one deformed hand. "And there's not much glory in that."

Dowling returned the microphone to its stand. He stood behind it and, with increased volume, continued speaking.

"And now here we are. We're handicapped! Handicapped, they say." His voice lowered slightly. "But what is a handicap? It's just a chance for a good honest fight. When I was a boy on the river, I fought with boys. When I became a man, I changed foes."

Nowhere was there a sound. Even the traffic outside the building seemed to have come to a stop. There was only the voice of Michael Dowling. He cleared his throat and pointed at the front row.

"The real fight starts and ends with how you feel about yourself. Long ago, I decided that I was a winner. I had to be if I wasn't going to let down my mother. I couldn't let... "

His right hand flew to his cheek. A small crystal tear, reflected in the spotlight, was erased with a quick movement. He breathed deeply.

"I couldn't let down my mother. She always wanted me to be somebody, to walk straight and tall. Believe me, as a boy with no legs, many times I wondered how I was ever going to walk straight and tall."

And now Dowling's voice became very strong; he seemed to be slightly angry. "NOBODY WAS GOING TO TELL ME THAT I WASN'T A WINNER!"

He backed off slightly. "Nobody was going to tell Michael Dowling he was a loser! Nobody! Not those doctors, or those county commissioners, not those grown-ups who pitied me, not those college kids. Nobody could tell me I was a loser. Because in my mind I knew I WAS A WINNER!"

He coughed. Fatigue was caressing his eyes.

"Handicap? There's only one handicap; the loss of the inner power of the mind. Why, you don't need hands, you don't need legs. You need courage! That's all. Our bodies, yeah, of course... but they aren't near as important as the human mind."

He chuckled a little now. "I've been told that a man may be worth a hundred thousand dollars a year from the neck up... and not worth a dollar a week from the neck down. It's the mind... the mind that has the most value."

He paused, brought out his handkerchief, wiped at the perspiration on his brow and lowered his voice.

"Affliction turns some into sponges; sponges that soak up self-pity. They never get anywhere."

"You want to see the strongest, sturdiest trees out on the plains? Well I'll show them to you. They're the ones, the great oak trees, that have been buffeted by the wind, by adversity. Tons of snow have been dumped on them. Bolts of lightning have seared their bark. But they remain standing to show the world what strength and integrity are all about."

"There are plenty of things worse than losing a part of your body. You may lose a part of your heart. When that happens, you become a real cripple. When you give-up, when you lose your desire to win, when there is no more fun in life, then you become a real cripple."

He pointed toward the rear door of the building and continued. "You can look out there on the avenue any day and see the real cripples. You can see it in their eyes. There is no sparkle. You can see it in the way they walk. Their walk is lifeless. They are crippled!" Dowling shook his head at the vision he had created within his own mind.

"If you want to pity someone, pity them."

"The Lord has been good to me." His voice was almost reverent. "I know now the luckiest day of my life was that day out there in Canby, Minnesota, when the doctors began to cut away. Right there, 14-years-old, without a mother to hold me, without a father, and without brothers and sisters, just a little dog named Silver." The memory was too vivid; a tear spilled over his eyelid. "Right there I told myself that I was going to be a winner, and that stupid, old blizzard wasn't going to ruin my life."

He wiped the tear away and continued.

"I made up my mind to do something. Not because of any great ability I had. I simply said I WILL, and I DID! You boys will do the same, because there is nobody that can tell you, you are losers! You know it, I know it, everyone in here knows that you are winners!"

Dowling was not the only one whose face was wet with tears. Not only in the front rows, but throughout the hall handkerchiefs were in motion. Men, women, big, small, lame and whole, wiped at faces and felt a burning sensation as they struggled to swallow.

They began to applaud.

In the second row two soldiers with crutches pulled themselves to their feet. With the padded crutch tops wedged under their arms, they clapped with the others. Then, more on the front rows, most with watery eyes, struggled to their feet. The men in wheelchairs held clapping hands high over their heads. It was their standing ovation.

Dowling stood silent. The noise filled the room. Five thousand and six hundred people were standing and clapping for him.

Suddenly the picture of that day, in Canby, returned. He was riding high in the saddle, bringing in the entire herd. He was proud. The feelings were the same. He smiled and tried to continue.

"Boys, the horse to bet on is the one with a handicap. He is handicapped because he is the best horse. You are the boys who can win the fight. Your handicap is God's greatest blessing, for you will begin to think, to work and to win now as you never would have tried before."

"It was said we would be friends when this night was over. Well, I've always believed that friends help each other. They believe in each other, and I believe you will understand me when I say..."

He was struggling with emotion as were his listeners, but his voice was strong.

One final time, Michael Dowling, the man who would die in a short time, wiped at a tear and looked at the front rows with a sincerity that would never be captured by the words of journalists reporting on the night's activities.

He spoke with all the strength and conviction he could pull from the unwavering spirit within his broken body.

"I know you'll understand me when I say, I feel sorry for cripples! I am not bluffing. I thank God I am not a cripple!"

"I THANK GOD WE'RE NOT CRIPPLES!   Thank you for being here."

And then Michael Dowling walked slowly off the stage,  but he was straight and tall.

# *EPILOGUE*

Dowling died of heart failure in a St. Paul Hospital, on April 25, 1921. He was 55-years-old. Businesses in Olivia, Minnesota, where the Dowling family home still stands, closed their doors on the day of the funeral. On handwritten signs, most offered a simple explanation for the closure: "We mourn our loss."

An estimated three thousand people, from all parts of the region, stood in the wind on the front lawn of the family home to hear the brief service. At Dowling's request, not a word was spoken in his praise.

Three clergymen representing different faiths each quoted scripture and talked of life and death. But their message was only a formality. Those who looked upon the casket, those who knew the man best, understood the real message.  It was the life of Michael John Dowling.

Late in Dowling's life the State of Minnesota founded a school for "crippled children" in Minneapolis.     In honor of Dowling and his achievements, the school was called "The Michael Dowling School for Crippled Children."    Dowling visited the school many times, motivating its students with success stories.   "The Michael Dowling School" continues to operate in Minneapolis at the corner of "Edmunds" and "Dowling" Streets, overlooking the Mississippi River.

"Courage Center" founded in part by Mrs. Jennie Bordewich Dowling and located in Golden Valley, Minnesota, offers hope and education to thousands of physically-challenged individuals each year.

This book is dedicated to the men, women and children who face challenges I've never known, but who inspire and motivate people like me each day.

**To the Michael Dowlings everywhere.**

-Lynn Lehmann
January-August, 1997
Renville & Yellow Medicine
Counties, Minnesota
Salt Lake City, Utah

*Special thanks to the following:*

*The Minnesota State Historical Society*
*St. Paul, Minnesota*

*Michael Prichard*
*(Michael Dowling's Grandson)*

*Norman W. Larson*
*(Professor at the University of St. Thomas, St. Paul, Minnesota)*

*Blair & Jean Younger*
*(Current owners of the Michael Dowling home in Olivia, Minnesota)*

*Kathy Jundt*
*(Courage Center, Golden Valley, Minnesota)*

*L.K. "Micky" Pearson & Brian Altman*
*(Dowling School, Minneapolis, Minnesota)*

*The staff at the Yellow Medicine County Courthouse*

*...and especially Kerry Lee*

*Also, a group of authors and publications who wrote about Michael Dowling many years ago:*

Irving Bacheller
John Culbert Faries
James Martin
Mary B. Mullett
Carl & Amy Narvested
Prudence Tasker Olsen
The American Magazine
The New York Sun
The New York Tribune
The Saturday Evening Post

Author's note: Dowling campaigned success-
fully for the election of President William
McKinley. Most observers believed Dowling
could have easily received a high-ranking,
diplomatic appointment for himself. Instead,
when asked if he would be willing to serve as
a foreign diplomat, he suggested the name of
his father-in-law, Henry Bordewich, the man
who had helped him persuade county
commissioners to send him to college.
President McKinley appointed the Civil War
veteran to the post of Consul General in
Norway. He died there, the country of his
birth, in 1912.


Jennie Bordewich Dowling was instrumental
in developing and operating summer camps
for handicapped children. Before Mrs.
Dowling's work such camps were virtually
unheard of. Her life, like her husband's, was
devoted to helping those who were challenged
with physical disabilities. She died in Minneapolis in 1943.

Michael Dowling was eventually reunited
with his father.  Dowling's oldest daughter,
Dorothy Prichard, recalls her grandfather,
John Dowling, visiting their home in Olivia,
Minnesota while she was a young girl.

At the time of the first printing of this book, in
late summer 1997, Dorothy- 98-years-old,
was still enjoying life in Minnesota.

Today, among the tall and dignified monuments and headstones in the Olivia, Minnesota, cemetery, sits a small concrete planter. It reads:

## MICHAEL J. DOWLING
### 1866 - 1921

It marks the final resting spot of the boy who fought his way past almost insurmountable obstacles to become the man who stood straight and tall.

## About the Author:

Lynn R. Lehmann has spent the majority of his life in broadcasting. He is the author of *Miracle at Midnight,* and creator and co-producer of the *Fox Television Network* series, *Beyond Belief: Fact or Fiction?*

He and his wife, Kerry, live in Salt Lake City, and are the parents of three sons.

The story of Michael Dowling is true. The author has endeavored to accurately portray the events, chronology, people, places and names that are the story of Michael Dowling. He, however, has added some minor, fictitious elements that he believes help to tell the story.

Schools and other organizations may order bulk quantities of this book at discounts by writing to:

QUIKREADPRESS
2106 Linden
SLC, UT. 84121

Comments to the author may be forwarded to the same address.